8 Projects ♥ Easy to Sew Kiss lock Bags & Masks

I0382409

This Book Belongs To

_____

_____

It's Sew Easy: Bags & Masks
Copyright © 2020 by Jacine Wang
All rights reserved.

No part of this product may be reproduced in any form, unless otherwise stated, in which case reproduction is limited to the use of the purchaser. The written instructions, photographs, designs, projects, and patterns are intended for the personal, noncommercial use of the retail purchaser and are under federal copyright laws; they are not to be reproduced by any electronic, mechanical, or other means, including informational storage or retrieval systems, for commercial use. Permission is granted to photocopy patterns for the personal use of the retail purchaser.

ISBN: 978-1-7333503-4-1 (eBook)
ISBN: 978-1-7333503-5-8 (Paperback)
Library of Congress Control Number: 2020925950

The information in this book is presented in good faith, but no warranty is given nor results guaranteed. Since the author and/or the publisher have no control over choice of materials of procedures, the author and/or the publisher assume no responsibility for any consequences arising from the information, advice or instructions given in this publication.

By purchasing this book, you agree not to share, upload elsewhere, or resell the pattern either as a digital download or printed pattern. You are prohibited from giving or selling any of the patterns in this book to a magazine, blog, or book publisher. You are not allowed modifying the pattern slightly and sell it as your own creation.

Readers are permitted to reproduce any of the items/patterns in this book for their personal use, or for the purposes of selling for charity, free of charge, or home industry and without the prior permission of the author. Any use of the items/patterns for commercial purposes is not permitted without the prior permission of the author. Properly attribute each item (and online listing) that is being made using the patterns in this book is welcome, but not required.

Attention Teachers: The author encourages you to use this book for teaching, subject to the restrictions stated above.

Attention Copy Shops: Please note the following exception - publisher and author give permission to photocopy pattern page for personal use only.

The author and/or publisher are not affiliated with or sponsored by the licensed fabrics used and presented in this book.

Photographs, illustrations, interior and cover designed by Jane J. Wang

Published in 2021 by EZ2Sew Design Studio, a division of EZ Shop & Design
            Plano, Texas USA

For further inspiration, visit website: www.ezshopdesign.com

Printed in the United States of America

10 9 8 7 6 5 4 3 2 1

8 Projects ♥ Easy to Sew Kiss lock Bags & Masks

It's Sew Easy
Bags & Masks

Jacine Wang

2Sew Design Studio

Table of Contents

Acknowledgements
Introduction

Essential Tools..1
Fabric & Interfacing..3
Hardware & Accessory....................................4
Basic Bag Construction..................................5
Project 1 - Bag: Madison..............................12
        Pattern..17~20
Project 2 - Bag: Lilliana..................................21
        Pattern..26~29
Project 3 - Bag: Violet....................................30
        Pattern..36~39
Project 4 - Mask: Aurora................................40
        Pattern..45~56
Project 5 - Mask: Baylee................................57
        Pattern..61~62
Project 6 - Mask: Blossom............................63
        Pattern..68~70
Project 7 - Mask: Lydia..................................71
        Pattern..75~82
Project 8 - Mask: Luna..................................83
        Pattern..87~94
About the Author

Acknowledgements

Writing a book about how to sew is much harder than sewing and designing patterns. None of this would have been possible without my family's support and encourage. And, the most important thing is the amazing feedback provided by the readers and supporters, encouraging me to continue to write more!

To my son, Johnathan: thank you for taking the time to read the draft and edit it for me. Editing is not an easy task, but you are so patient with me.

Even though I am not affiliated with or sponsored by the trademark owner of the fabrics, I still want to thank those who created and designed the beautiful fabrics that I used and presented in my book.

Introduction

At the beginning of the pandemic, many places didn't have enough PPE (Personal Protective Equipment) for frontline health workers who are risking their lives to keep the rest of us safe. During this difficult time, wearing a mask became the so-called "new normal". We must carry around a mask, hand sanitizer and alcohol wipes with us, on top of our usual belongings (keys, wallet, phone and other essential items) whenever we go out. The mask also functions as a "new fashion accessory" in our daily lives during the pandemic. Wearing a mask is a must during these times, and it could be fashionable like any other accessory.

I've sewn many masks for my family and friends over the past few months since the pandemic and I am very happy to see them wearing it, not only to protect them, but also being stylish.

This book features 3 storage bags that can hold essential items (masks, filters, hand sanitizer and alcohol wipes) when you need to go out, and 5 different styles of masks which have an insert pocket for the filter. Each style contains several different sizes that can fit most of the people.

"It's Sew easy" to make these "bags" and "masks" included in this book. Join me and have fun sewing these projects!

12.25.2020

Disclaimer: This book is not about who, what, when, where, why and how to wear a mask. For more information, please follow the WHO (World Health Organization) and local health organization's guidelines.

TOOLS

Essential Tools

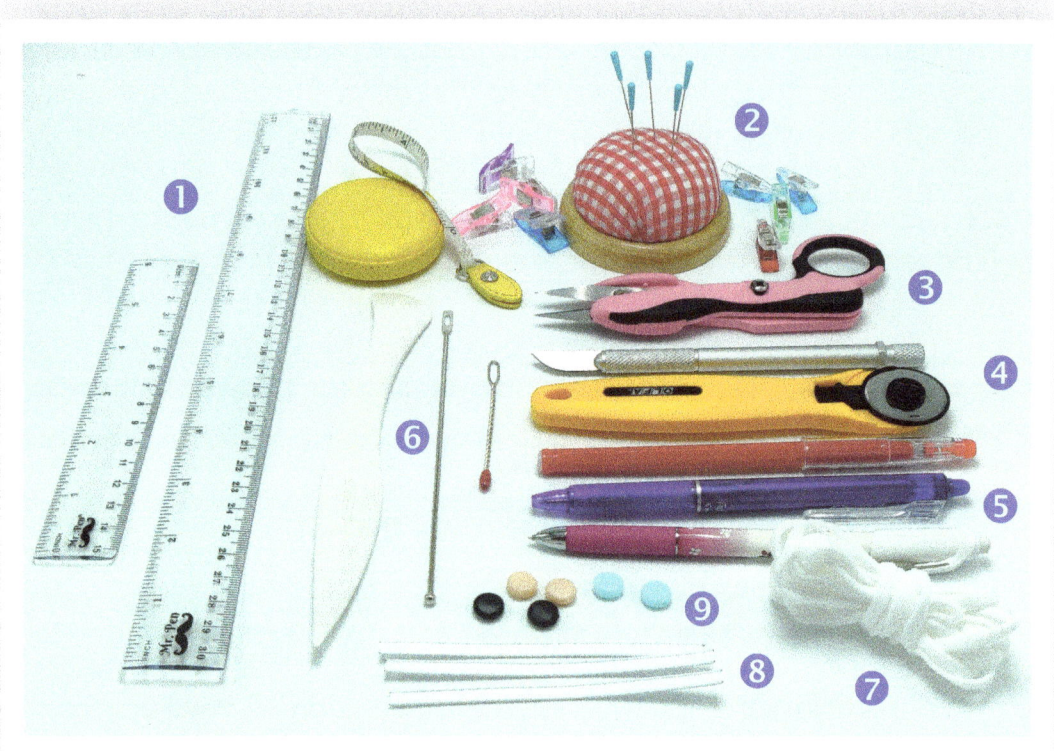

1. Clear Ruler, Tape Measure, Seam Gauge
2. Sewing Pins, Clips, Pin Cushion
3. Thread snips, Seam Ripper, Awl
4. Rotary Cutter, Craft Knife, Cutting Mat
5. Fabric Marking Pencils, Tailor's Chalk, Erasable Gel Pens
6. Point Turner, Bodkin
7. 1/5" (0.5cm) Elastic
8. 3.9" (10cm) Nose Wire Strip
9. Elastic Cord Buckle/lock

Hand Sewing Needle
Thimble

TOOLS

Essential Tools

Craft Shears
A good pair of craft scissors can be used to cut the patterns.

Fabric Cutting Shears
Fabric cutting shears are used for cutting fabric.

Pinking Shears
Pinking shears have blades with serrated edges. They leave a zigzag pattern after cutting. They are useful for trimming off excess material on a curved seam to reduce the bulk.

Seam Roller
This tool is very useful for pressing the seams flat without using iron.

Compass
An instrument for drawing circles and arcs.

Iron and Ironing Board

Sewing Machine
You don't need a fancy or complicated sewing machine. Any sewing machine that can sew a straight line will get the job done.

FABRIC & INTERFACING

★ For both *Mask* and *Kiss lock Storage Bag*: Light to medium weight cotton or quilting cotton for main and lining.

Cotton (light weight) *Quilting Cotton* (light to medium weight)

★ For *Mask*: No interfacing needed.

★ For *Kiss lock Storage Bag*: Check below.

❶❷❸ used for: **Exterior**
❹ used for: **Interior**;

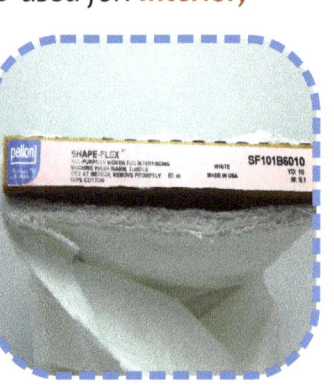

❶ *Heat & Bond High Loft Iron-On Fusible Fleece*
❷ *Pellon 987F Fusible Fleece*
❸ *Pellon TP971F Fusible Thermola*
❹ *Pellon SF101 Shape-Flex Woven Fusible Cotton*

📢 Always follow the manufacturer's directions for applying any interfacing to the fabric.

📢 Test before applying to any main fabric. You can also mix and match two or three different kinds of interfacing onto the fabric.

HARDWARE & ACCESSORY

Measuring conversion rate: 1 inch = 2.54 cm (1" * 2.54 = 2.54 cm)
SIZE - **W**: *Frame width*; **H**: *Frame height* (**NOT** *including the kiss lock*); **P**: *Perimeter of the frame*;
SHAPE - **R**: *Round*; **Rect**: *Rectangle*; MATERIAL: **M**e**T**al;
Used for: the <<*Pattern name*>> used in this book;

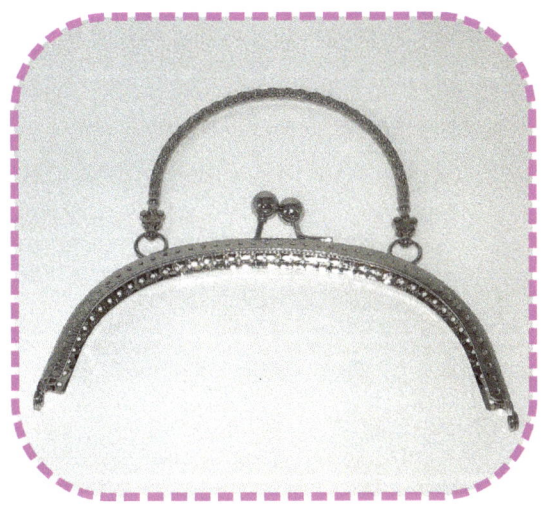

W: 6.5" (16.5 cm); **H**: 3.35" (8.5 cm)
P: 9.65" (24.5 cm)
Shape: **R** / **MT**
Used for: The *Madison*

W: 5" (13 cm); **H**: 3.25" (8 cm)
P: 10.83" (27.5 cm)
Shape: **Rect** / **MT**
Used for: The *Violet*

W: 5.9" (15 cm); **H**: 2.16" (5.5 cm)
P: 9.5" (24 cm)
Shape: **Rect** / **MT**
Used for: The *Lilliana*

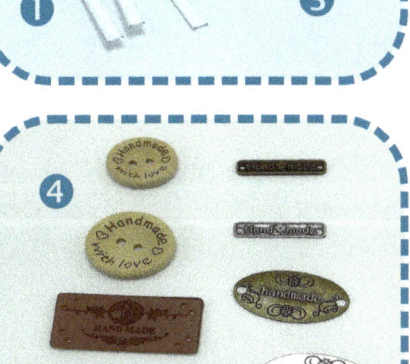

❶ 3.9" (10cm) Nose Wire Strip
❷ Elastic Cord Buckle/Lock
❸ 1/5" (0.5cm width) Elastic Band
❹ Handmade Tag

*** Please allow 1/16"~1/8" (0.15~0.3 cm) differences at all measurements above. ***

BASIC BAG CONSTRUCTION

Some of the elements of bag construction that will be introduced in this chapter include curved seams, slip pockets, 3-D pockets, and installing the purse frame.

Construct a Curved Seam

1 Trace the Pattern. Trace the pattern with **NO** seam allowance by using chalk or erasable pen on the wrong side of both connecting fabrics. This will be the seam line and will help you focus on the fabric while sewing, regardless if you are hand sewing or using a sewing machine.

2 Match the center markings. Match the center markings, then use clips or pins to hold them in place. Place the piece with the curved seam under the piece with the straight seam, right side facing each other.

3 Sew the center to hold them in place (Optional, but Recommended). You might want to sew the center of the straight seam first to hold both pieces in place.

4 Cut slits in curves. Near the curved areas where both pieces will be joined, cut a few slits on the top piece with the straight seam, so that the fabric will become more flexible to match the bottom fabric with curved seams.

5 Match the rest of the Markings. Match the side markings on both sides, use pins or clips to hold them all the way around.

6 Sew all the way around. If you did step 3, sew halfway until you meet the straight seam, and then finish the other half. Otherwise, sew all the way around.

7 Repeat. Repeat the same steps above on other side of the piece, if needed, depending on the pattern.

BASIC BAG CONSTRUCTION

Construct the Slip Pocket - Style A

1 *Right side facing each other.* Place both the pocket Main and Lining fabric Right side facing each other. Align all the markings, top and bottom, especially the center.

2 *Sew the top of the pocket.* Sew along the curved line by using the seam allowance of your choice at the top of the pocket ONLY, do NOT sew all the way around.

3 *Make notches.* Use pinking shears to make notches at the curved seam allowance.

4 *Turn Right side out.* Flip the joined pieces Right side out and align all the markings at the bottom if there are any, especially the centers. Smooth the curved seam with your finger tip, using the iron to press the pocket flat if needed.

5 *Topstitching.* Top stitch at the top of the pocket after flipping the pocket piece Right side out.

6 *Attach to the base piece.* Attach the pocket piece to the base piece, align all the markings, especially the centers. Baste stitch the pocket to the base piece all the way around (except the top).

6

BASIC BAG CONSTRUCTION

Construct the Slip Pocket - Style B

1 **Get both the pocket Main and Lining pieces ready to connect.** Place the pocket Main and Lining pieces Right sides facing each other. Align the center markings.

2 **Sew both top and bottom edges.** Sew only the top and bottom edges by using the seam allowance of your choice and leave both side edges open.

3 **Turn Right side out.** Turn the pocket piece Right side out through one of the side edges. Press well if necessary.

4 **Topstitch before attaching to the base piece.** Top stitch the top edge ONLY by using the seam allowance 1/16" (2 mm).

5 **Connect the pocket piece to the base piece.** Place the pocket Main fabric Right side facing up on top of the base piece, align all the centers, the pocket top, right, and left corners, and the bottom center to the marking on the base piece.

6 **Attach to the base piece.** Sew three sides to close the pocket bottom and attach to the base piece (please refer to the marking at the "Pocket" pattern).

BASIC BAG CONSTRUCTION

Construct the Slip Pocket - Style C

1 **Get both the pocket Main and Lining pieces ready to connect.** Place the pocket Main and Lining pieces Right sides facing each other. Align the center markings.

2 **Sew all the way around** and *leave an opening* at the bottom straight seam for turning the pocket piece Right side out.

3 **Turn the pocket piece Right side out** through the bottom opening. Press well if necessary.

4 **Topstitch the top edge ONLY before attaching to the base piece** by using the seam allowance 1/16" (2 mm).

5 **Attach the pocket piece to the base piece.** Place the pocket Main fabric facing up on top of the base piece, align the centers. Sew three sides to attach (please refer to the pattern).

Construct the 3-D Pocket

 *I*f you see this special marking at the bottom of the pattern piece, this will be the 3-D Pocket piece. Let's understand what this special marking means before starting to construct it.

Understand the Special Marking

*P*inch marking ❶ and fold it over on top of marking ❷. Align both markings and use clips to hold them in place.

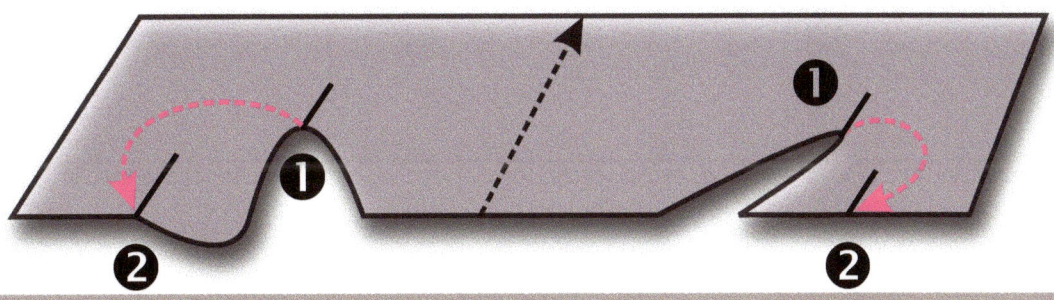

BASIC BAG CONSTRUCTION

Construct the 3-D Pocket (continue)

1 **Follow Steps 1 to 5 from constructing the "Slip Pocket".** Please refer to the section **"Construct the Slip Pocket - Style A"**.

2 **Create a casing for the elastic.** After top stitching at the top of the pocket, sew a straight line away from the top stitching seam to create a casing (1/16" wider than the width of the elastic you are using) for inserting the elastic.

3 **Feed the elastic through the casing.** Mark the desired width on the elastic as the pattern instruction. Attach the bodkin or a large safety pin to the edge of one end of the elastic and insert through the casing.

4 **Adjust the gathers evenly and hold both ends in place.** Gently feed the elastic through one side of the casing, use pin or clip to hold the tail in place once reaching the marking. Adjust the gathers as you go. Stretch the elastic until you match the width markings on both ends.

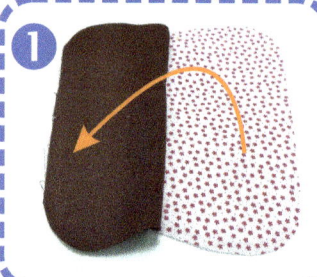

5 **Make 3-D folds at the bottom of the pocket.** Please refer to the previous page **"Understand the Special Marking"** to make 3-D folds at the bottom of the pocket on both sides.

6 **Attach to the base piece.** Align the bottom markings at both the pocket and base pieces. Use pins or clips to hold both pieces in place. Topstitch both pieces to join them together by using 1/16" (2 mm) seam allowance, and then trim the excess elastic at both sides.

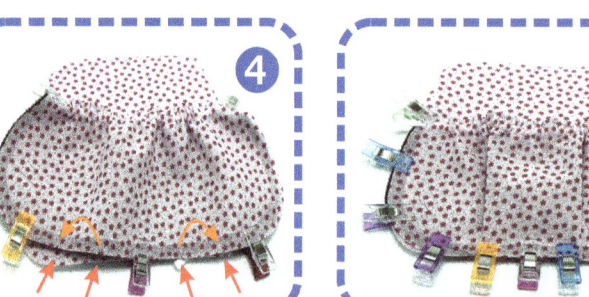

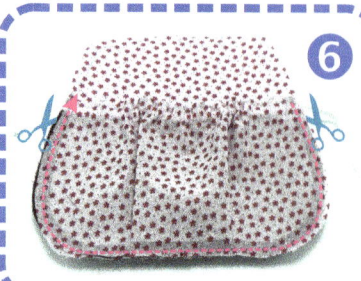

BASIC BAG CONSTRUCTION

Install the Sew-in Purse Frame

*S*ince installing the sew-in style purse frame is a bit challenging, it won't be an issue if you practiced slowly and patiently. Please refer to my other books, "<u>Sew Amazingly Cute</u>" and "<u>Sew Amazingly Elegant</u>", for more details of installation.

1 Starting from the inside of the 1st hole, pull the needle through the fabric and all the way through to the outside.

2 From the outside, push the needle through the 2nd hole.

3 Loop the needle back into the 1st hole again from inside.

4 Push the needle through the 2nd hole again, ending with the thread on the inside.

The steps above are called "Back" stitching, securing the thread. We will do these steps again when we reach the last 2 holes on the same side of the purse frame.

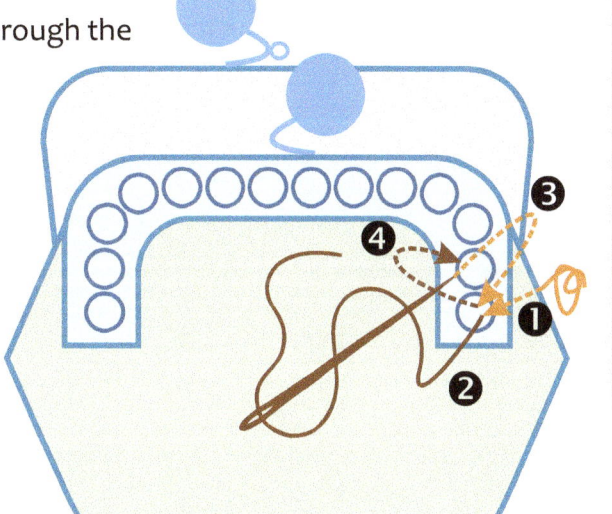

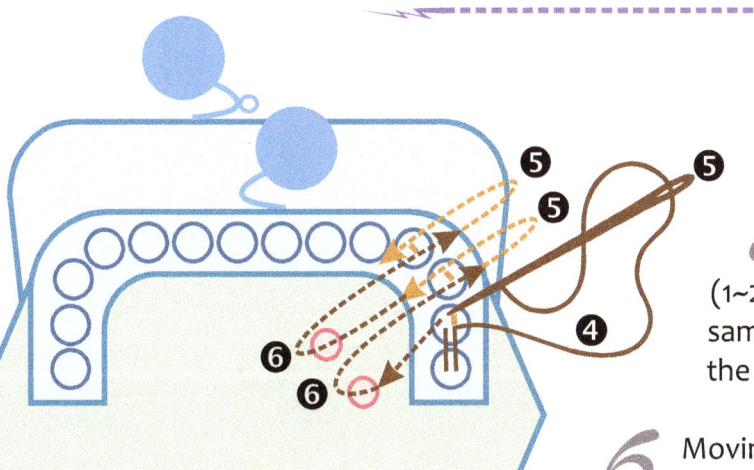

*A*fter step 4, the needle should be on the inside of the 2nd hole.

5 Now, place the needle next to the last stitch about 1/16" (1~2mm) away from it, then from the same hole, pull the needle through to the outside.

6 Moving to the next hole, push the needle through to the inside.

From inside the 3rd hole, repeat these 2 steps until reaching the last 2 holes.

BASIC BAG CONSTRUCTION

Sew-in Purse Frame (continue)

*A*fter repeating steps 5 and 6 several times, finally, we reach last two holes.

7 Now, the needle should be on the outside of the 2nd to last hole. Push the needle into the last hole from the outside.

8 We need to secure the thread and do the "Back" stitch, like we did with the first 2 holes. Loop the needle back into the 2nd to last hole again, ending up on the outside.

9 Push the needle back into the last hole, ending up on the inside. Move on to step 10, or repeat steps 8 and 9 one more time.

10 Tie a knot and cut the remaining thread tail.

Repeat steps 1~10 with the other side of the frame. Remove Basting stitches if you used them.

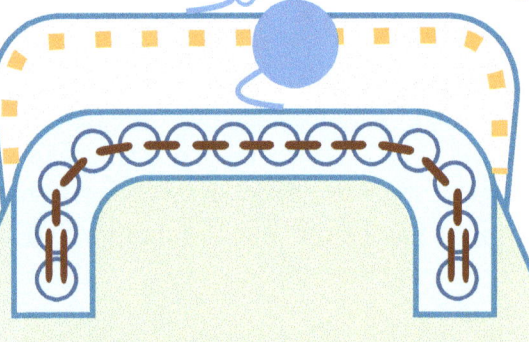

By using the Slip Stitch to install the frame, it will leave small dots in the interior and dashes on the exterior.

*B*y using the **Slip Stitch** to install the frame to the purse piece, the interior will appear like dots under the frame and the exterior will have dashes that connect each hole.

If you are interesting in using other stitches, like the **Running Stitch** or **Back Stitch** to install the frame, please check the book "<u>Sew Amazingly Cute</u>" for more information.

11

MADISON

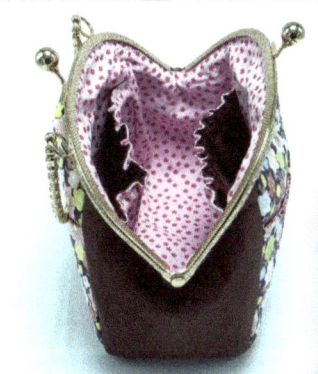

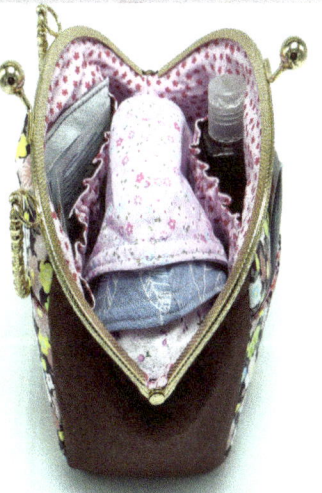

Bag: Madison

cm: 20 (Top W) x 14 (Bottom W), 13 (H) x 6 (D)
inch: 8" x 5.5", 5" x 2.36"
* Top W: the widest part; H: not including the frame;

PREPARATION

PREPARING ALL THE MATERIALS

✂ For NON-Directional Fabrics

Exterior/Interior/Interfacing:

- **Main/Lining** fabric (Pattern B) - "Front & Back" x 2; "Side Gusset & Bottom" x 1;

- **Interfacing** (Pattern A) - "Front & Back" x 2; "Side Gusset & Bottom" x 1;

Pocket/Interfacing: Each pocket is constructed in pairs (Main x 1, Lining x 1); you may make 2 exterior slip pockets and 2 interior 3-D pockets

- **Exterior Pocket (Style A)**: main x 1, lining x 1; interfacing x 1;

- **Interior 3-D Pocket**: main x 1, lining x 1; interfacing x 1; 16 cm (6.5") elastic x 1;

✂ For Directional Fabrics

- **"Front & Back"**: the same as non-directional fabrics;

✂ "Side Gusset & Bottom":

☞ [Option 1] Fold "Side Gusset & Bottom" (Pattern A) in half, add seam allowance all the way around (Pattern B) x 2;

☞ [Option 2] "Side Gusset" (Pattern B) x 2; "Bottom" (Pattern B) x 1;

 *Tip: Do **NOT** apply the interfacing until all the "Side Gusset & Bottom" pieces are connected together.*

 NOTE: Add seam allowance before cutting any fabric. No seam allowance needed for cutting the interfacing, unless using a sew-in interfacing.

★ **Pattern A** - the original pattern which has "NO Seam Allowance"
★ **Pattern B** - add "Seam Allowance" of your choice (1/4", 3/8" or 1/2") to Pattern A

DIRECTIONS

 There are three parts of this piece: Main/Exterior, Lining/Interior and an optional - Exterior (Main)/Interior (Lining) Pockets. Add seam allowance around the patterns before cutting any fabric. Prepare all the materials and apply interfacing to the fabric.

Construct the Exterior

1 **Construct the exterior pocket.** Please refer to the chapter **"Basic Bag Construction"**, the section **"Construct the Slip Pocket - Style A"**.

2 **Complete the exterior construction.** Please refer to the chapter **"Basic Bag Construction"**, the section **"Construct a Curved Seam"** to complete the exterior construction.

Construct the Interior

1 **Construct the interior pocket.** Please refer to the chapter **"Basic Bag Construction"**, the section **"Construct the 3-D Pocket"**.

2 **Complete the interior construction.** Do the same as how you construct the exterior to complete the interior construction.

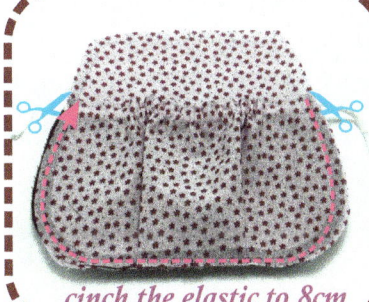

cinch the elastic to 8cm

Bag: Madison

DIRECTIONS

Complete the Purse piece

1. **Get Main and Lining pieces. Connect both pieces.** You should have both Main and Lining pieces ready to complete the purse piece. Place the Main piece (Right side out) into the Lining piece (Wrong side out), with the Right sides of both pieces facing each other. Align all center markings.

   Use chalk or erasable pen to draw the seam line on the Wrong side of the Lining before sewing.

2. **Sew all the way around the top and leave an opening** to connect both pieces with the seam allowance of your choice. Use Pinking Shears to trim the excess or cut notches on the curved seam. Clip the tops of both side seams.

   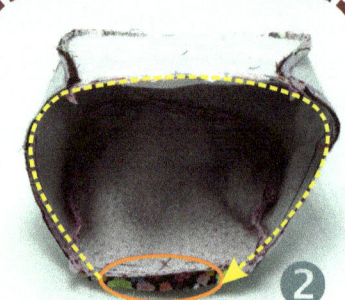

3. **Turn Right side out.** Turn the whole purse piece Right side out through the opening. Use your finger tip or something pointy (but not sharp) to round out the top curved seam.

4. **Press well.** Use an iron to press the purse piece with a bit of steam to remove wrinkles if necessary.

5. **Fold the opening seam allowance inward to the Wrong side.** Use clips or pins to hold it in place.

6. **Topstitching.** Top stitch all the way around the top edge by using 1/16" (2 mm) seam allowance.

   Do NOT use a seam allowance larger than 1/8" (3 mm), even though the top edge will be under the frame; using a seam allowance smaller than 1/8" will work well.

7. **Mark all 4 centers.** Press well if needed. Use chalk or erasable pen to mark all 4 centers.

DIRECTIONS

Install the purse frame

 Install the purse frame. Get the correct size and shape purse frame ready to install to the completed purse piece.

Please refer to the Chapter "Basic Bag Construction", the section "Install the Sew-in Purse Frame".

Special Marking on the pattern

 The **double half circle** marking indicates the place where to join/connect the fabric.

★ For **NON-Directional** fabric: **FOLD** the fabric in half and line up the double half circle marking along the folded edge. Add seam allowance all the way around, except the edge with the double half circle. Cut the fabric as ONE piece. (Figure 2)

★ For **Directional** fabric: Add seam allowance all the way around on the pattern, and then cut two pieces of the fabric. Connect two pieces of fabric at the special marking with the seam allowance of your choice. Now, the fabric becomes ONE piece. (Figure 3)

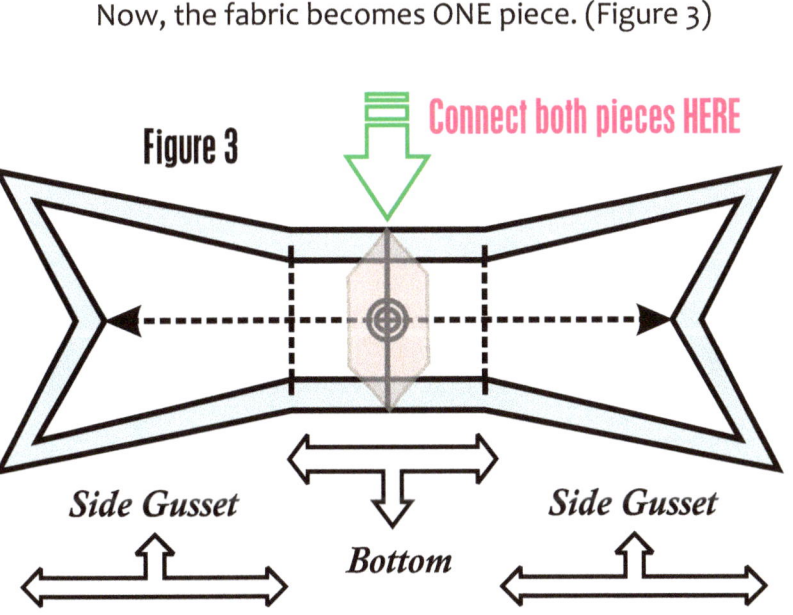

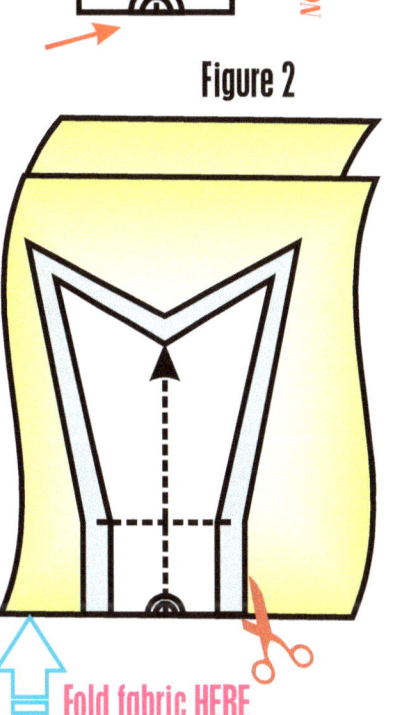

PATTERN

[Pattern]: Madison

✦ **NOTE:** *The attached pattern has NO seam allowances included. Add seam allowance of your choice (1/8", 1/4", 1/2" or 0.7 cm, 1 cm, 1.25 cm) before cutting any fabric or sewing!* ☺

Printing Instructions

*P*lease make sure your printer's scaling is set to "none," "actual size" or "100%". Do NOT check the "scale to fit paper size" option. Once the pattern is printed out, make sure it printed correctly. Check the "1 inch (3 cm) Square" and it should measure 1" x 1" (3 cm x 3 cm). If the square is not the correct size, check the printer settings again.

3cm

1"

The Madison
6.5" x 3.35" (16.5 x 8.5 cm)
III_R_VI
Pocket
(Exterior Front & Back)
No Seam Allowance

Copyright © 2020 EZ Shop & Design, EZ2Sew Design Studio All rights reserved.

PATTERN

Bag: Madison

1"

The Madison
6.5" x 3.35" (16.5 x 8.5 cm)
III_R_VI
Front & Back
No Seam Allowance

3cm

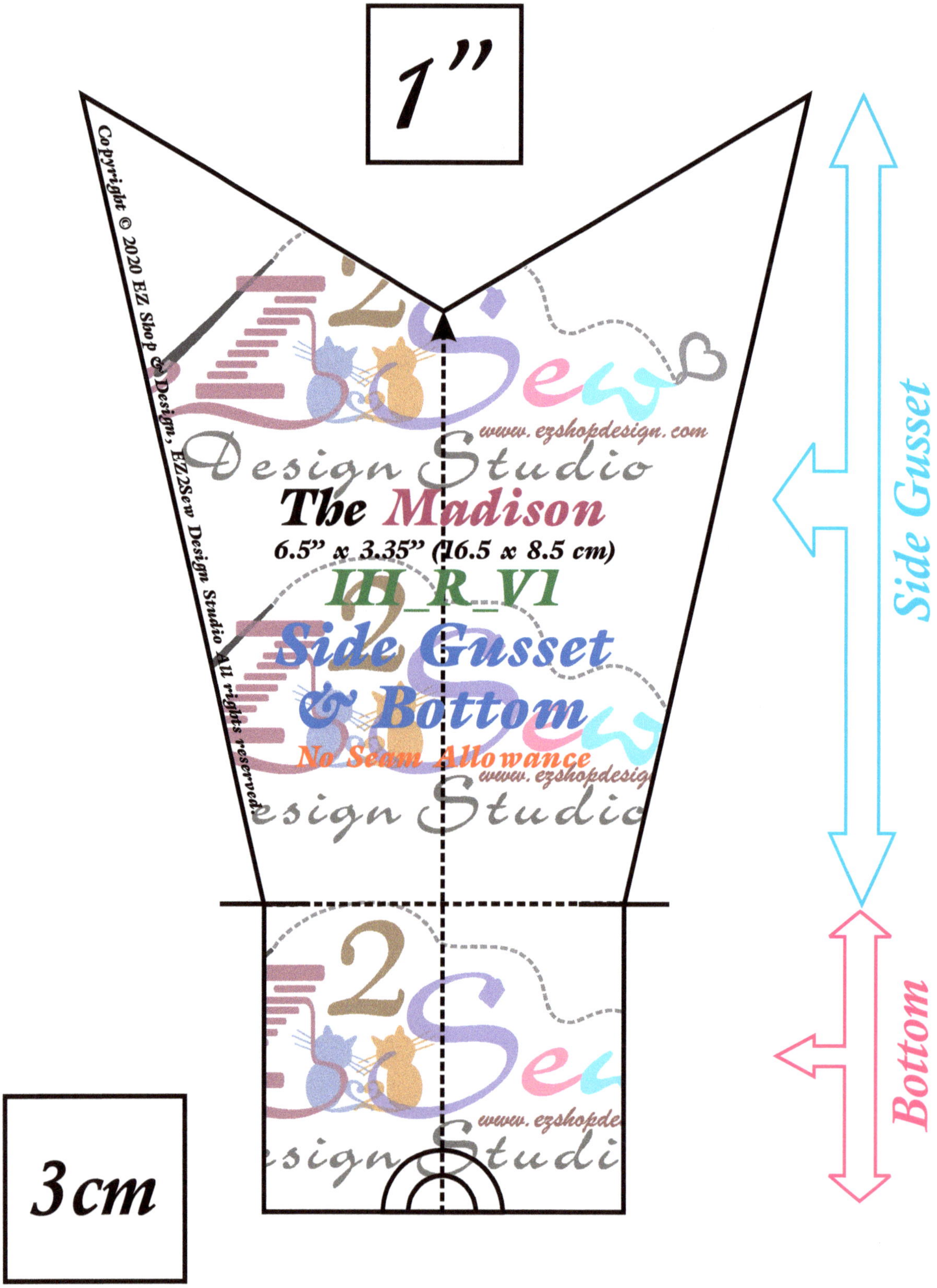

PATTERN

1"

The Madison
6.5" x 3.35" (16.5 x 8.5 cm)
III_R_V1
Side Gusset & Bottom
No Seam Allowance

Side Gusset

Bottom

3cm

Bag: Madison

PATTERN

1"

3 cm

The Madison
6.5" x 3.35" (16.5 x 8.5 cm)
III_R_VI
3-D Pocket
(Interior Front & Back)
No Seam Allowance

Bag: Madison

20

LILLIANA

Bag: Lilliana

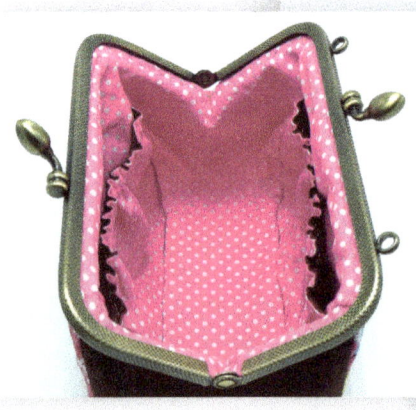

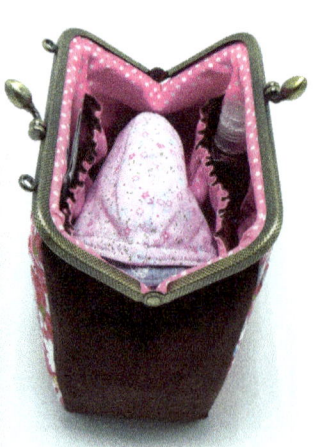

cm: 21.5 (Top W) x 17 (Bottom W), 12 (H) x 6 (D)
inch: 8.5" x 6.75", 4.75" x 2.375"

Top W: the widest part; H: not including the frame;

PREPARATION

PREPARING ALL THE MATERIALS

✂ For NON-Directional Fabrics

Exterior/Interior/Interfacing:

- **Main/Lining** fabric (Pattern B) - "Front & Back" x 2; "Side Gusset & Bottom" x 1;

- **Interfacing** (Pattern A) - "Front & Back" x 2; "Side Gusset & Bottom" x 1;

Pocket/Interfacing: Each pocket is constructed in pairs (Main x 1, Lining x 1); you may make 2 exterior slip pockets and 2 interior 3-D pockets

- **Exterior Pocket (Style A)**: main x 1, lining x 1; interfacing x 1;

- **Interior 3-D Pocket**: main x 1, lining x 1; interfacing x 1; 20 cm (8") elastic x 1;

✂ For Directional Fabrics

- **"Front & Back"**: the same as non-directional fabrics;

✂ "Side Gusset & Bottom":

☞ [Option 1] Fold "Side Gusset & Bottom" (Pattern A) in half, add seam allowance all the way around (Pattern B) x 2;

☞ [Option 2] "Side Gusset" (Pattern B) x 2; "Bottom" (Pattern B) x 1;

✎ *Tip: Do **NOT** apply the interfacing until all the "Side Gusset & Bottom" pieces are connected together.*

✎ NOTE: Add seam allowance before cutting any fabric. No seam allowance needed for cutting the interfacing, unless using a sew-in interfacing.

> ★ **Pattern A** - the original pattern which has "NO Seam Allowance"
> ★ **Pattern B** - add "Seam Allowance" of your choice (1/4", 3/8" or 1/2") to Pattern A

DIRECTIONS

 There are three parts of this piece: Main/Exterior, Lining/Interior and an optional - Exterior (Main)/Interior (Lining) Pockets. Add seam allowance around the patterns before cutting any fabric. Prepare all the materials and apply interfacing to the fabric.

Construct the Exterior

1 **Construct the exterior pocket.** Please refer to the chapter **"Basic Bag Construction"**, the section **"Construct the Slip Pocket - Style A"**.

2 **Complete the exterior construction.** Please refer to the chapter **"Basic Bag Construction"**, the section **"Construct a Curved Seam"** to complete the exterior construction.

attach the "Side Gusset & Bottom" to the "Front & Back"

turn the main piece Right side out

DIRECTIONS

Construct the Interior

1 **Construct the interior pocket.** Please refer to the chapter **"Basic Bag Construction"**, the section **"Construct the 3-D Pocket"**.

2 **Complete the interior construction.** Do the same as how you construct the exterior to complete the interior construction.

sew the top edge of the pocket

flip to the Right side

feed the elastic through the casing

cinch the elastic to 9cm

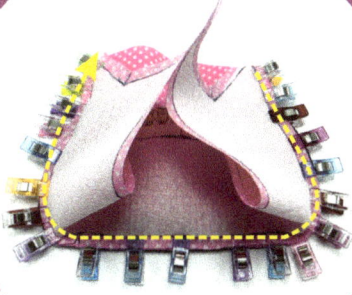

Complete the Purse piece

1 **Get Main and Lining pieces. Connect both pieces.** You should have both Main and Lining pieces ready to complete the purse piece. Place the Main piece (Right side out) into the Lining piece (Wrong side out), with the Right sides of both pieces facing each other. Align all center markings.

 Use chalk or erasable pen to draw the seam line on the Wrong side of the Lining before sewing.

Main piece
Lining piece
①

DIRECTIONS

Complete the Purse piece

2 **Sew all the way around the top and leave an opening** to connect both pieces with the seam allowance of your choice. Use Pinking Shears to trim the excess or cut notches on the curved seam. Clip the tops of both side seams.

3 **Turn Right side out.** Turn the whole purse piece Right side out through the opening. Use your finger tip or something pointy (but not sharp) to round out the top curved seam.

4 **Press well.** Use an iron to press the purse piece with a bit of steam to remove wrinkles if necessary.

5 **Fold the opening seam allowance inward to the Wrong side.** Use clips or pins to hold it in place.

6 **Topstitching.** Top stitch all the way around the top edge by using 1/16" (2 mm) seam allowance.

✏️ *Do NOT use a seam allowance larger than 1/8" (3 mm), even though the top edge will be under the frame; using a seam allowance smaller than 1/8" will work well.*

7 **Mark all 4 centers.** Press well if needed. Use chalk or erasable pen to mark all 4 centers.

Install the purse frame

1 **Install the purse frame.** Get the correct size and shape purse frame ready to install to the completed purse piece.

✏️ *Please refer to the Chapter "Basic Bag Construction", the section "Install the Sew-in Purse Frame".*

PATTERN

[Pattern]: Lilliana

★ **NOTE:** *The attached pattern has **NO** seam allowances included. Add seam allowance of your choice (1/8", 1/4", 1/2" or 0.7 cm, 1 cm, 1.25 cm) before cutting any fabric or sewing!* ☺

Printing Instructions

Please make sure your printer's scaling is set to "none," "actual size" or "100%". Do NOT check the "scale to fit paper size" option. Once the pattern is printed out, make sure it printed correctly. Check the "1 inch (3 cm) Square" and it should measure 1" x 1" (3 cm x 3 cm). If the square is not the correct size, check the printer settings again.

Bag: Lilliana

3cm

1"

The Lilliana
5.9" x 2.16" (15 x 5.5 cm)
III_Rect_V1
Pocket
(Exterior Front & Back)
No Seam Allowance

Copyright © 2020 EZ Shop & Design, EZ2Sew Design Studio All rights reserved.

PATTERN

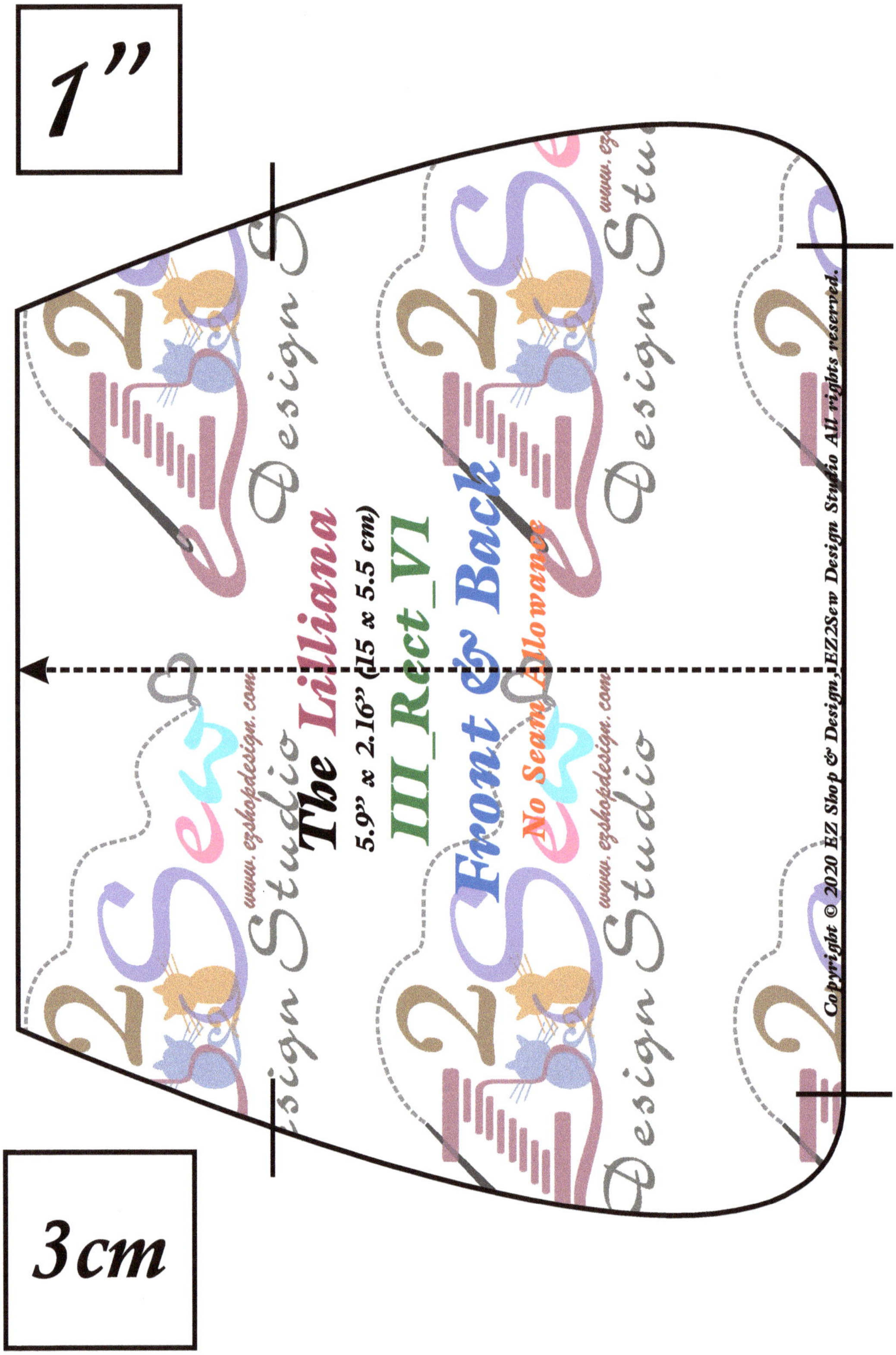

Bag: Lilliana

1"

The Lilliana
5.9" x 2.16" (15 x 5.5 cm)
III_Rect_V1
Front & Back
No Seam Allowance

3 cm

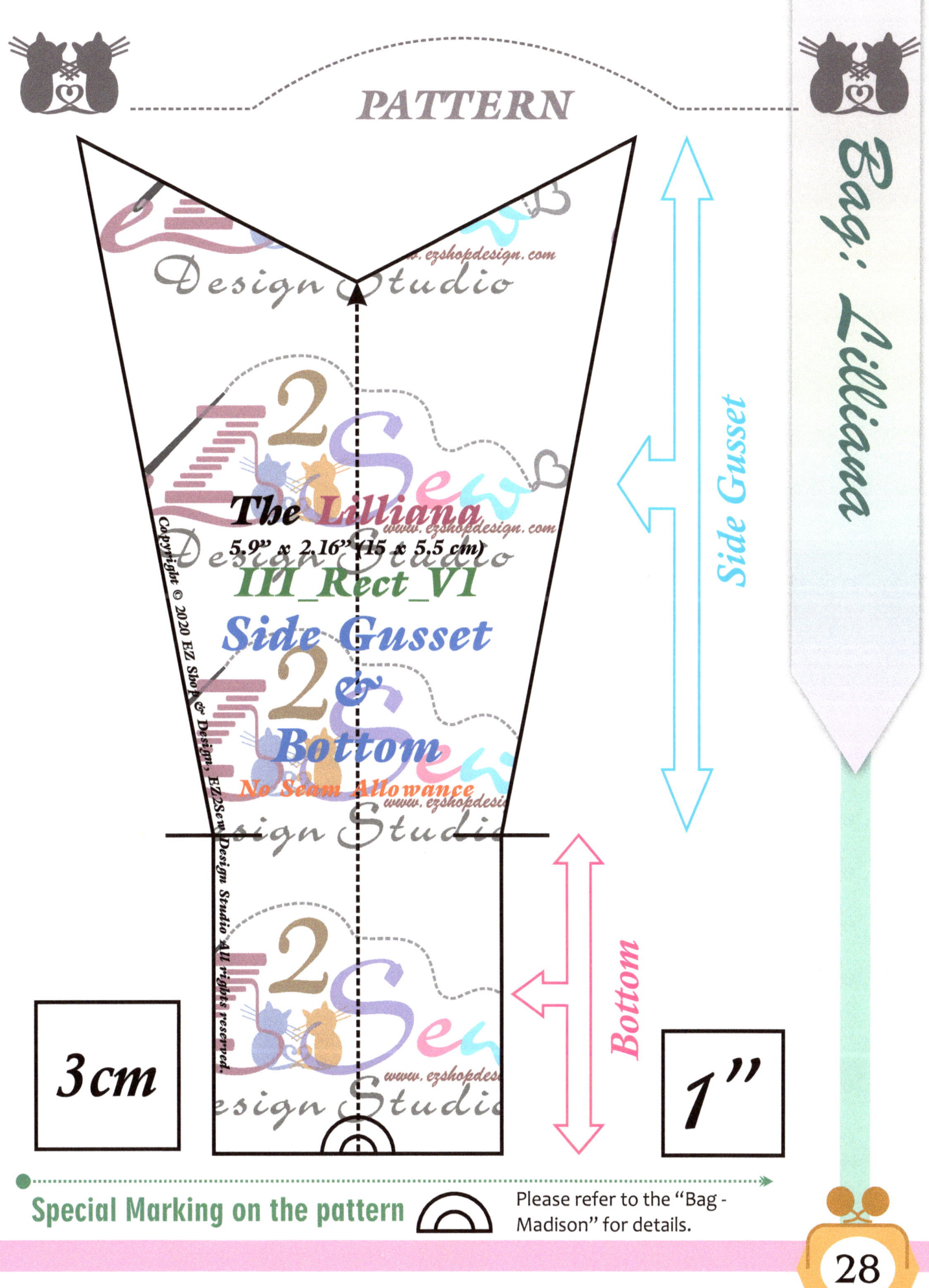

PATTERN

Bag: Lilliana

1"

3cm

The Lilliana
5.9" x 2.16" (15 x 5.5 cm)
III Rect VI
3-D Pocket
Interior Front & Back
No Seam Allowance

Copyright © 2020 EZ Shop & Design, EZ2Sew Design Studio. All rights reserved.

29

VIOLET

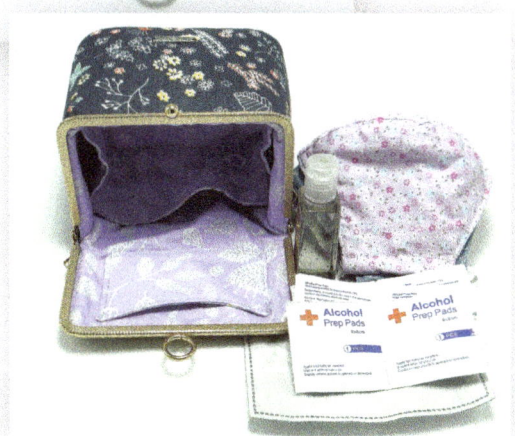

cm: 13 (Top W) x 9 (H) x 8 (D)
inch: 5 1/8" x 3.5" x 3.15"
* Top W: the widest part; H: not including the frame;

Bag: Violet

PREPARATION

PREPARING ALL THE MATERIALS

✂ For NON-Directional Fabrics

Exterior/Interior/Interfacing:

- **Main/Lining** fabric (Pattern B) - "Front + Side Gusset" x 1; "Top + Back + Bottom" x 1;

- **Interfacing** (Pattern A) - "Front + Side Gusset" x 1; "Top + Back + Bottom" x 1;

Pocket/Interfacing: Each pocket is constructed in pairs (Main x 1, Lining x 1);

- **Top Pocket (Style B)**: main x 1, lining x 1; interfacing x 1;

- **Back Pocket (Style C)**: main x 1, lining x 1; interfacing x 1;

- **3-D Pocket**: main x 1, lining x 1; interfacing x 1; 20 cm (8") elastic x 1;

✂ For Directional Fabrics

- Make sure the fabric is facing correct the direction, cut more than one piece and connect them together if necessary.

 *Tip: Do **NOT** apply the interfacing until all the pieces are connected together.*

 NOTE: Add seam allowance before cutting any fabric. No seam allowance needed for cutting the interfacing, unless using a sew-in interfacing.

> ★ **Pattern A** - the original pattern which has "NO Seam Allowance"
> ★ **Pattern B** - add "Seam Allowance" of your choice (1/4", 3/8" or 1/2") to Pattern A

Reference

DIRECTIONS

 There are several parts of this piece: Main/Exterior, Lining/Interior and Interior/Lining Pockets. Add seam allowance around the patterns before cutting any fabric. Prepare all the materials and apply interfacing to the fabric.

Construct the Interior

1 **Construct the interior pocket.** Please refer to the chapter *"Basic Bag Construction"*, the section *"Construct the Slip Pocket - Style B and Style C"*.

2 **Place Style B & C pockets onto the base piece.** Place *the* Style C pocket at the center of the top part of the *"Top + Back + Bottom"* piece. Place the Style B pocket at the center part of the *"Top + Back + Bottom"* piece. Please check the alignment markings on the pattern piece *"Top + Back + Bottom"*.

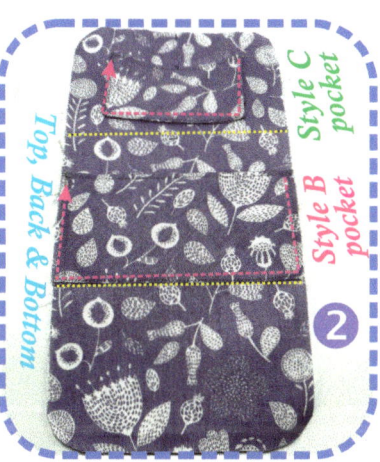

3 **Construct the interior 3-D pocket.** Please refer to the chapter *"Basic Bag Construction"*, the section *"Construct the 3-D Pocket"*. Place the 3-D pocket at the *"Front + Side Gusset"* piece. Divided the pocket into 3 sections.

  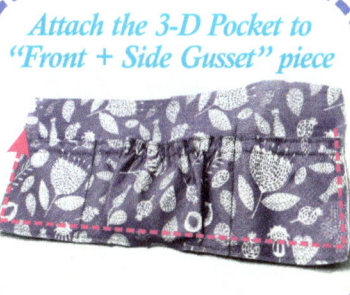

4 **Connect both "Top + Back + Bottom" and "Front + Sides" together.** Place the *"Front + Side Gusset"* piece horizontally on top of the *"Top + Back + Bottom"* piece, align at the centers and Right sides facing each other. Sew the shorter side of the *"Front + Side Gusset"* piece to connect both pieces together (please refer to the photo), using the seam allowance of your choice.

DIRECTIONS

Construct the Interior

5 **Complete the interior construction.** Please refer to the chapter **"Basic Bag Construction"**, the section **"Construct a Curved Seam"** and photos here to complete the interior construction.

Construct the Exterior

1 **Complete the exterior construction.** Do the same steps 4 and 5 as how you construct the interior to complete the exterior construction and refer to the photos below.

Find the center of the "Front+Side Gusset" piece and attach a tag/label.

Turn Right side out

DIRECTIONS

Bag: Violet

Complete the Purse piece

1 **Get Main and Lining pieces. Connect both pieces.** You should have both Main and Lining pieces ready to complete the purse piece. Place the Main piece (Right side out) into the Lining piece (Wrong side out), with the Right sides of both pieces facing each other. Align all center markings.

 Use chalk or erasable pen to draw the seam line on the Wrong side of the Lining before sewing.

2 **Sew all the way around the top and leave an opening** to connect both pieces with the seam allowance of your choice. Cut notches on the curved seam.

3 **Turn Right side out.** Turn the whole purse piece Right side out through the opening. Use your finger tip or something pointy (but not sharp) to round out the curved seam.

4 **Press well.** Use an iron to press the purse piece with a bit of steam to remove wrinkles if necessary.

5 **Fold the opening seam allowance inward to the Wrong side.** Use clips or pins to hold it in place.

6 **Topstitching.** Top stitch all the way around the top edge by using 1/16" (2 mm) seam allowance.

 Do NOT use a seam allowance larger than 1/8" (3 mm), even though the top edge will be under the frame; using a seam allowance smaller than 1/8" will work well.

7 **Mark all 4 centers.** Press well if needed. Use chalk or erasable pen to mark all 4 centers.

34

DIRECTIONS

Install the purse frame

1 **Install the purse frame.** Get the correct size and shape purse frame ready to install to the completed purse piece.

 Please refer to the Chapter "Basic Bag Construction", the section "Install the Sew-in Purse Frame".

Special Marking on the pattern

 The **diamond** shape marking indicates where you join/connect the pattern pieces together.

Figure 1

★ *Half diamond* (Figure 1):

❶ Print 2 copies of the same pattern piece.

❷ Cut out both copies and turn one of the pattern pieces to the reverse side (Figure 2).

❸ Line up both pieces to form the diamond.

❹ Use clear tape to connect both pieces together.

❺ The new pattern will be Pattern A (Figure 3) which has NO seam allowance. Add seam allowance of your choice all the way around to make the Pattern B before cutting any fabric.

Figure 2

Figure 3

** NOT an actual size of the pattern. Do NOT use it for cutting the fabric. **

PATTERN

[Pattern]: Violet

✯ **NOTE:** *The attached pattern has **NO** seam allowances included. Add seam allowance of your choice (1/8", 1/4", 1/2" or 0.7 cm, 1 cm, 1.25 cm) before cutting any fabric or sewing!* ☺

Printing Instructions

Please make sure your printer's scaling is set to "none," "actual size" or "100%". Do NOT check the "scale to fit paper size" option. Once the pattern is printed out, make sure it printed correctly. Check the "1 inch (3 cm) Square" and it should measure 1" x 1" (3 cm x 3 cm). If the square is not the correct size, check the printer settings again.

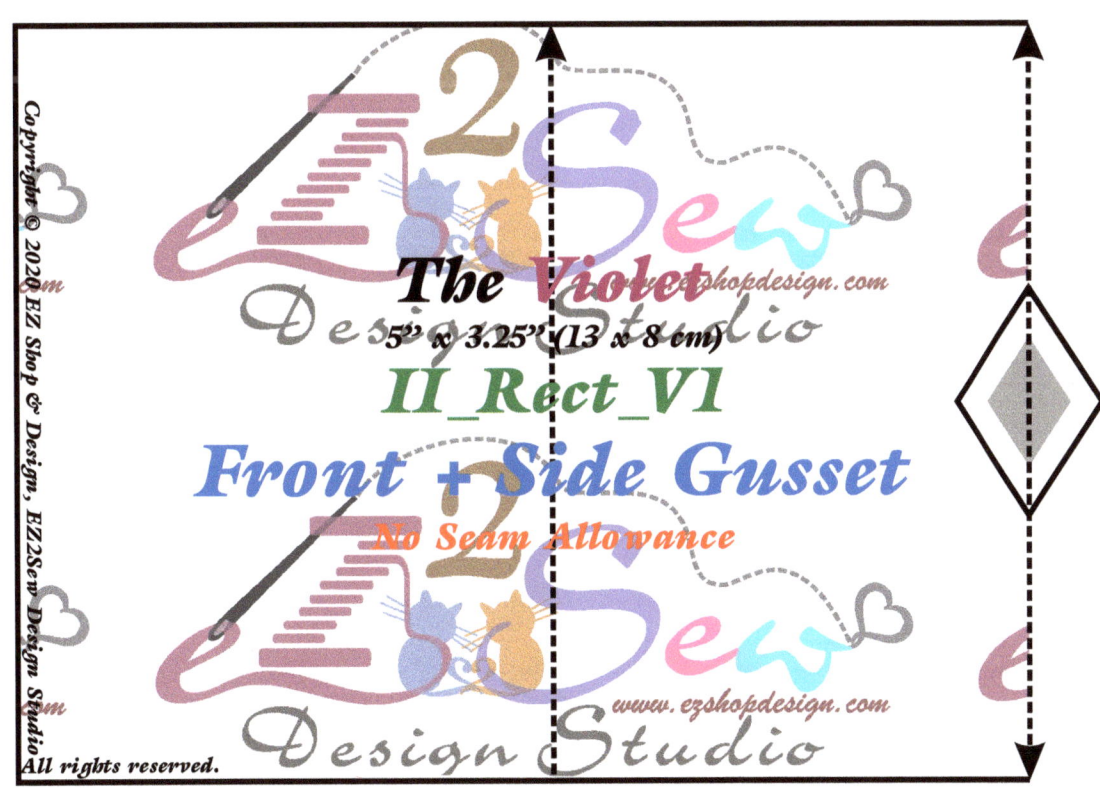

The Violet
5" x 3.25" (13 x 8 cm)
II_Rect_V1
Front + Side Gusset
No Seam Allowance

3cm   1"

PATTERN

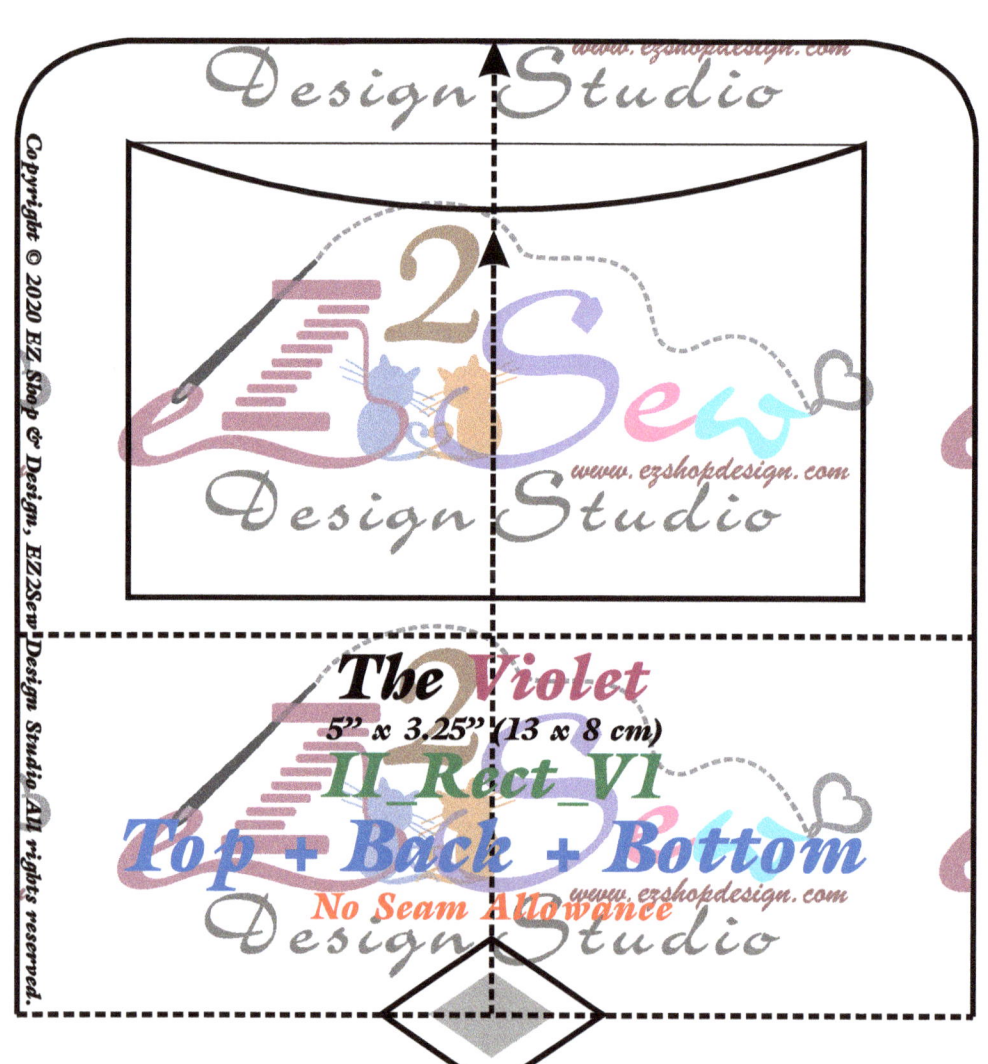

1"

The Violet
5" x 3.25" (13 x 8 cm)
II_Rect_V1
Top + Back + Bottom
No Seam Allowance

3cm

PATTERN

Bag: Violet

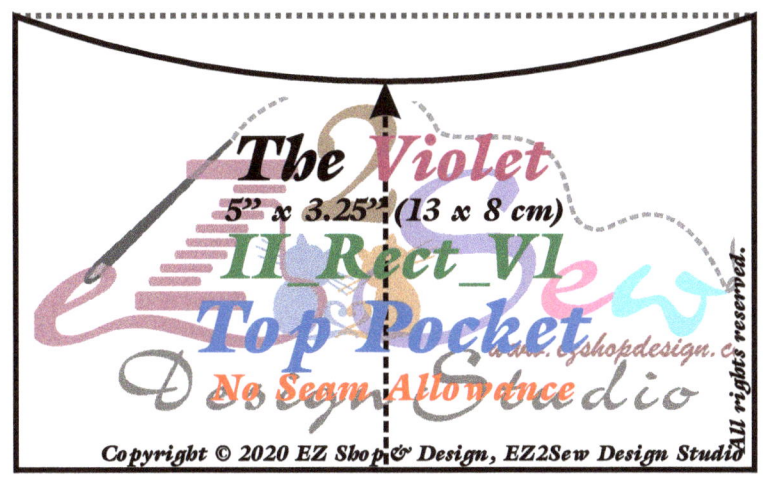

The Violet
5" x 3.25" (13 x 8 cm)
II_Rect_V1
Top Pocket
No Seam Allowance

| 3cm | 1" |

The Violet
5" x 3.25" (13 x 8 cm)
II_Rect_V1
Back Pocket
No Seam Allowance

PATTERN

Bag: Violet

1"

3cm

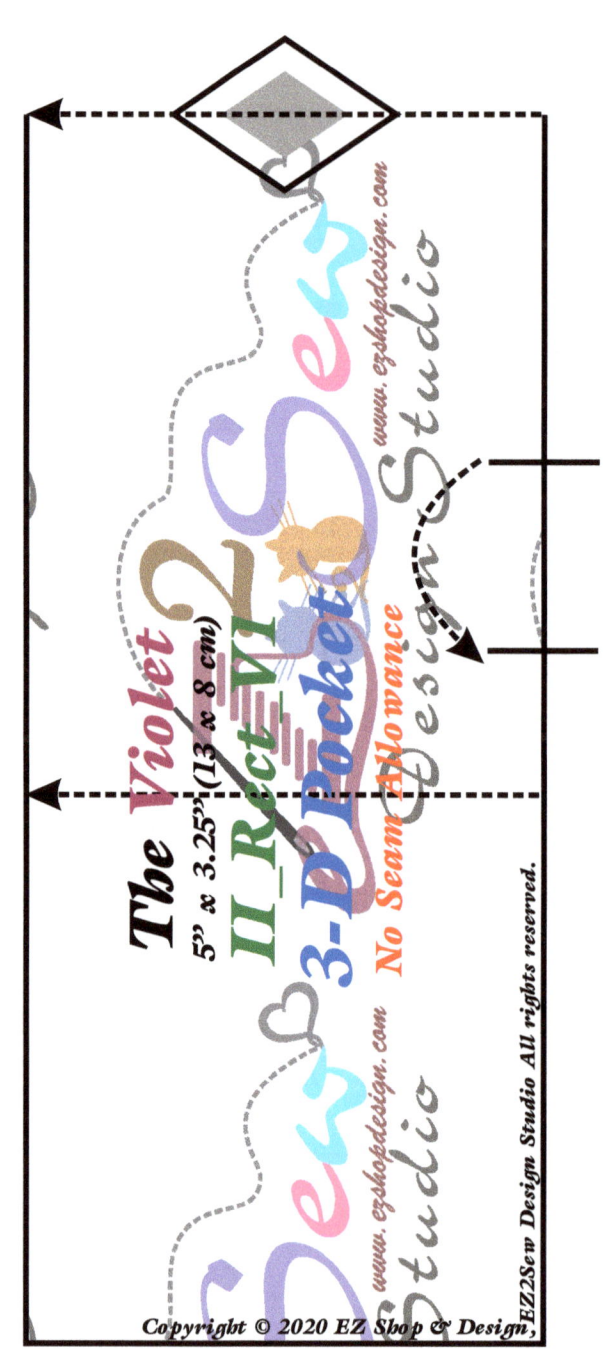

The Violet
5" x 3.25" (13 x 8 cm)
II_Rect_VI
3-D Pocket
No Seam Allowance

AURORA

Mask: Aurora

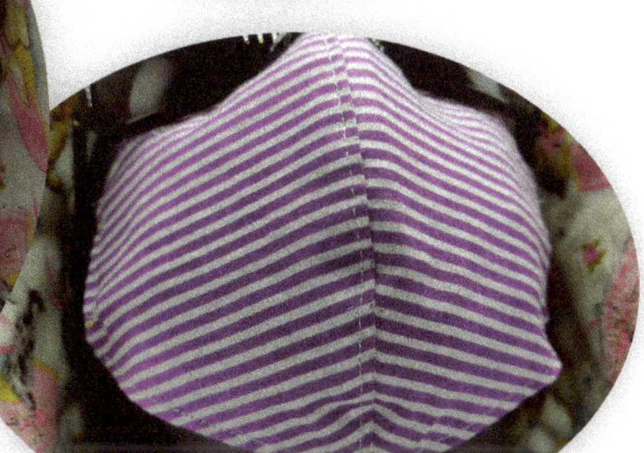

PREPARATION

PREPARING ALL THE MATERIALS

✂ **For NON-Directional Fabrics**

Exterior/Interior:

- **Main** fabric - "Main" x 2;
- **Lining** fabric - "Lining" x 2;
- **Insert** fabric - "Insert" x 2;

🔧 **HARDWARE & ACCESSORY:** 10cm (3.9") Nose Wire Strip x 1; 20cm x 0.5cm (8" L x 0.2" W) Elastic x 2.

✂ **For Directional Fabrics**

- The same as non-directional fabrics; Make sure they are in the correct direction.

✍ **NOTE:** Add seam allowance of your choice before cutting any fabric. No interfacing needed for making "Aurora" mask.

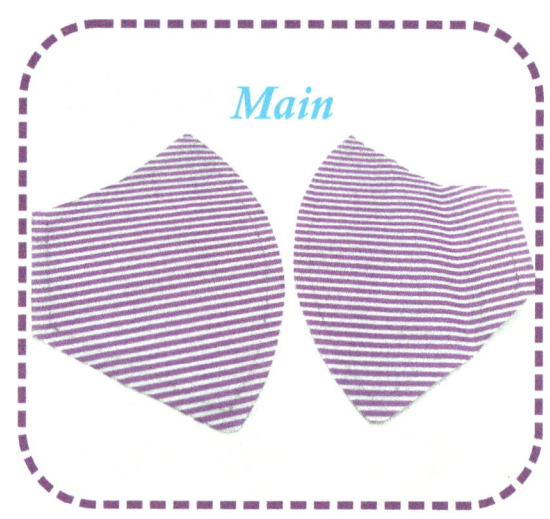

★ **Pattern A** - the original pattern which has *"NO Seam Allowance"*
★ **Pattern B** - add *"Seam Allowance"* of your choice (1/4", 3/8" or 1/2") to Pattern A

Mask: Aurora

DIRECTIONS

Construct the "Aurora" Mask

1 Sew the Lining raw edge. Double fold the taller side of the "Lining" piece to the Wrong side, the same width as the seam allowance and sew to hide the raw edge. Do the same on the other "Lining" piece.

2 Sew the Insert raw edge. Double fold the straight side of the "Insert" piece to the Wrong side, the same width as the seam allowance and sew to hide the raw edge. Do the same on the other "Insert" piece.

3 Connect both "Insert" pieces. Place both "Insert" pieces Right sides facing each other, sew the curved seam by using the seam allowance of your choice. Fold the seam allowance to either side. (Optional) Top stitch the connected "Insert" piece from the Right side, 2mm away from the center seam. Snip the seam allowance from the Wrong side if necessary.

4 Connect both "Main" pieces. Do the same as you connect both "Insert" pieces.

Mask: Aurora

42

DIRECTIONS

Construct the "Aurora" Mask

5 **Connect all the pieces together.** Get the connected "Main", the connected "Insert" and two "Lining" pieces ready to connect them all together. Place the "Insert" piece on top of the "Main" piece, Right sides facing each other, align the center. Then, place the "Lining" piece on each side of the "Insert" piece, Right side facing the Right side of the "Main" piece, align the markings on both sides. (please refer to the photo and pattern).

6 **Sew all the way around leave 4 openings.** Sew all the way around using the seam allowance of your choice and leave four openings at the corners. Don't forget to back stitches at each beginning and end (please refer to the photo and pattern markings).

7 **Turn Right side out and Top stitch.** Make a few clips on the curved seam. Turn the whole piece Right side out through the opening. Use your finger tip or something pointy (but not sharp) to round out the curved seam and four openings at corners. Top stitch all the way around, except those four openings at corners, using 2mm (1/16") seam allowance (please refer to the photo).

DIRECTIONS

Construct the "Aurora" Mask

8 **Make a casing.** Mark 5cm (2") away from the center at the top of the mask, sew a casing about 2mm (1/16") wider than the wire strip away from the top stitching seam. Feed the Nose Wire Strip through the casing (please refer to the photo).

9 **Feed the elastic cord through the openings.** Use the bodkin to feed one end of the elastic cord through one of the openings and do the same as the other end, then tie a knot or use a cord buckle (lock). Do the same on the other side (please refer the photos below).

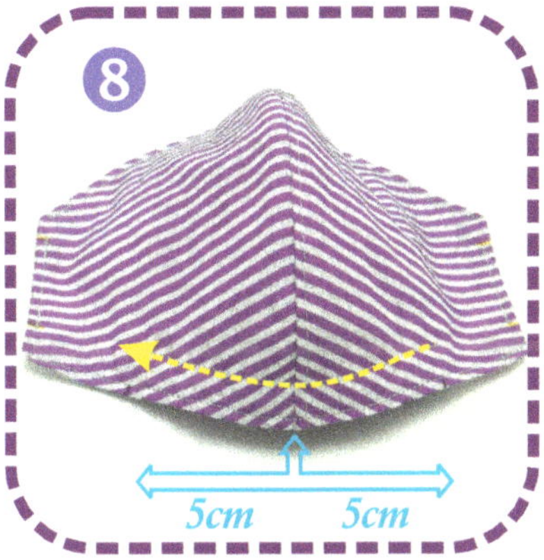

Mask: Aurora

44

PATTERN

[Pattern]: Aurora

✯ **NOTE:** The attached pattern has **NO** seam allowances included. Add seam allowance of your choice (1/8", 1/4", 1/2" or 0.7 cm, 1 cm, 1.25 cm) before cutting any fabric or sewing! ☺

✯ **NOTE:** Fold the fabric in half, Right side facing together, add seam allowances all the way around the pattern, and then cut 2 pieces of each pattern (Main, Insert and Lining). Please make sure the fabric is in correct direction before cutting.

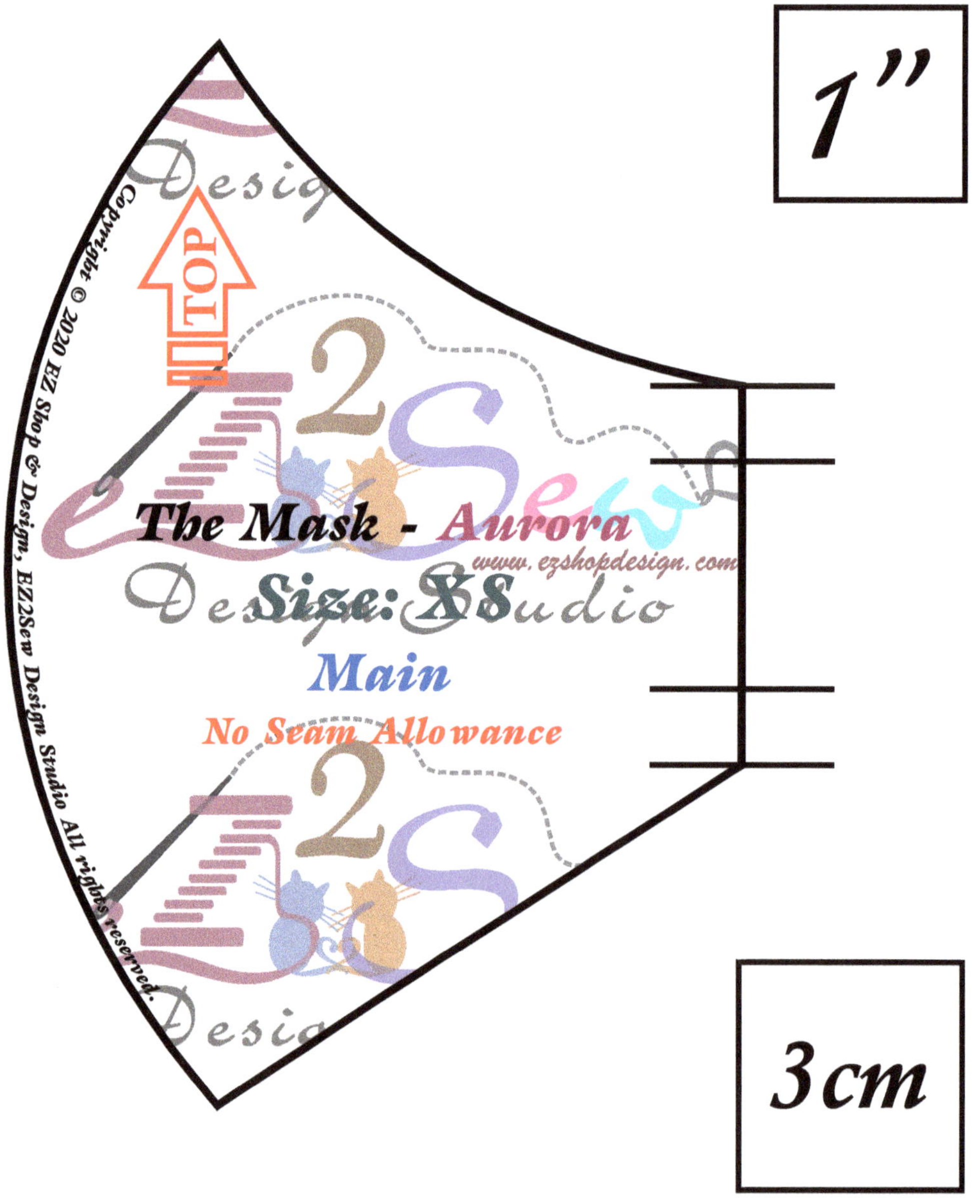

Mask: Aurora

TOP

The Mask - Aurora
Size: XS
Main
No Seam Allowance

1"

3cm

PATTERN

3cm

1"

Mask: Aurora

*P*lease make sure your printer's scaling is set to "none," "actual size" or "100%". Do NOT check the "scale to fit paper size" option. Once the pattern is printed out, make sure it printed correctly. Check the "1 inch (3 cm) Square" and it should measure 1" x 1" (3 cm x 3 cm). If the square is not the correct size, check the printer settings again.

PATTERN

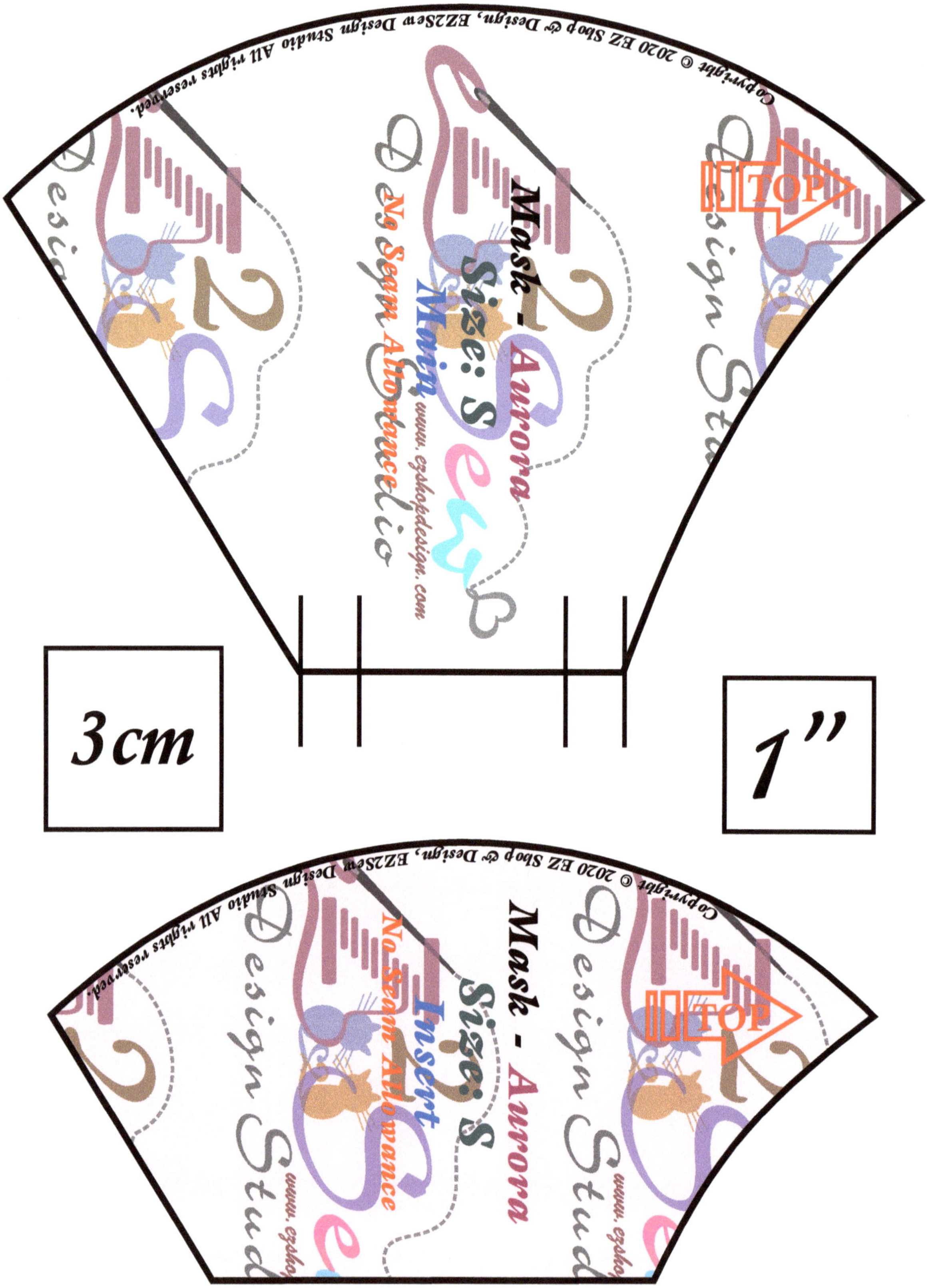

Mask: Aurora

Mask - Aurora
Size: S
Main
No Seam Allowance

3cm   1"

Mask - Aurora
Size: S
Insert
No Seam Allowance

PATTERN

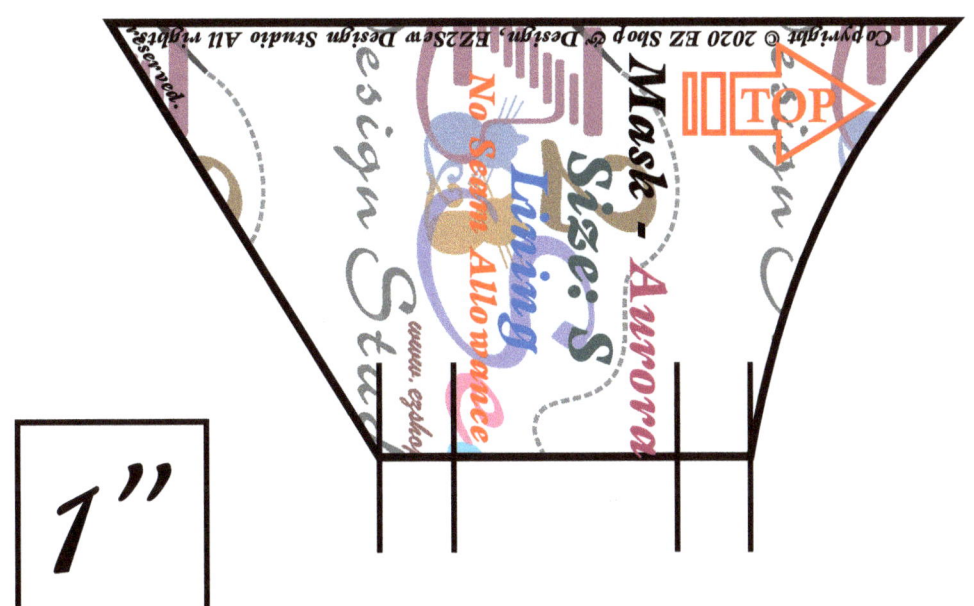

Mask: Aurora

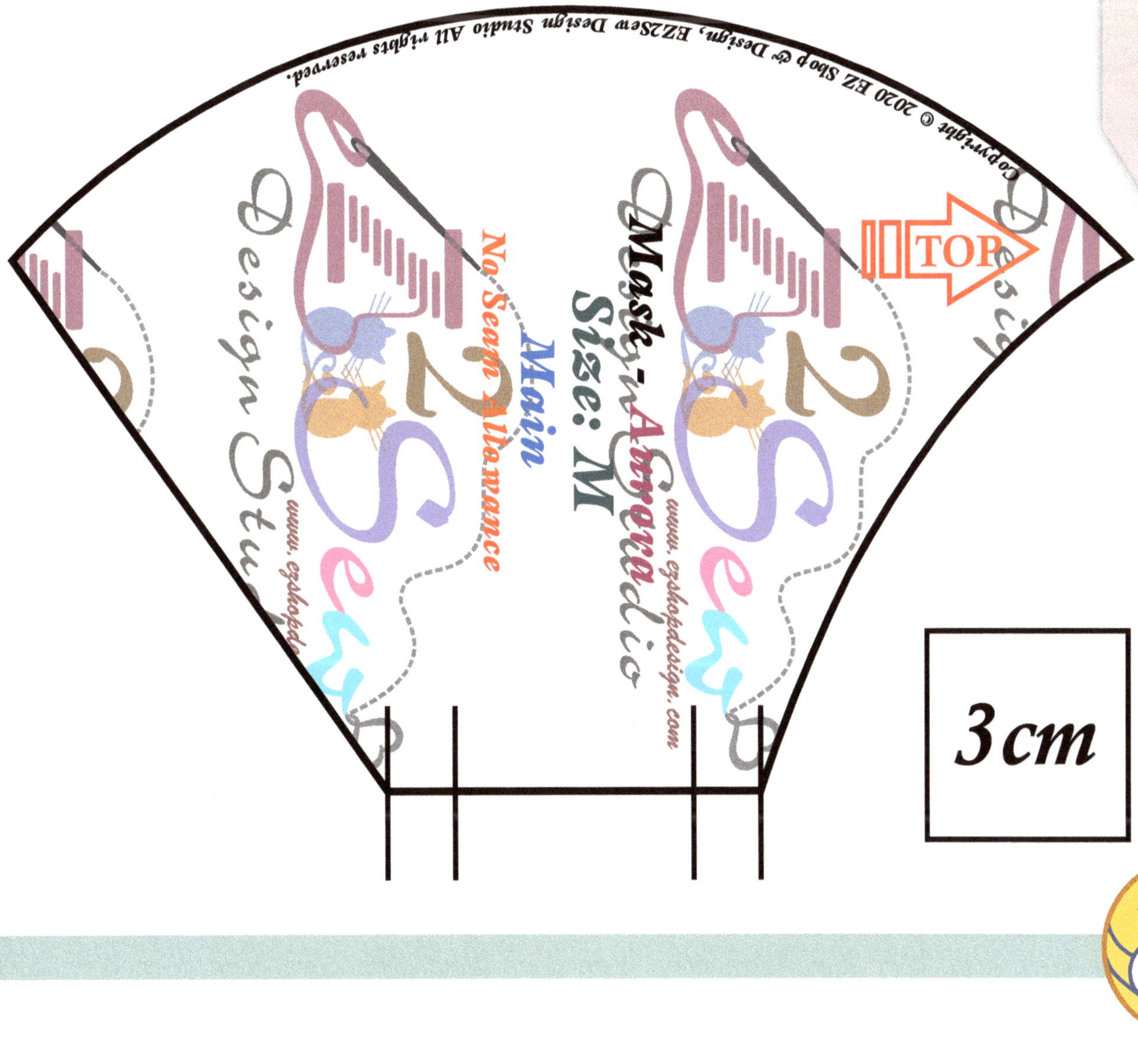

PATTERN

Mask: Aurora

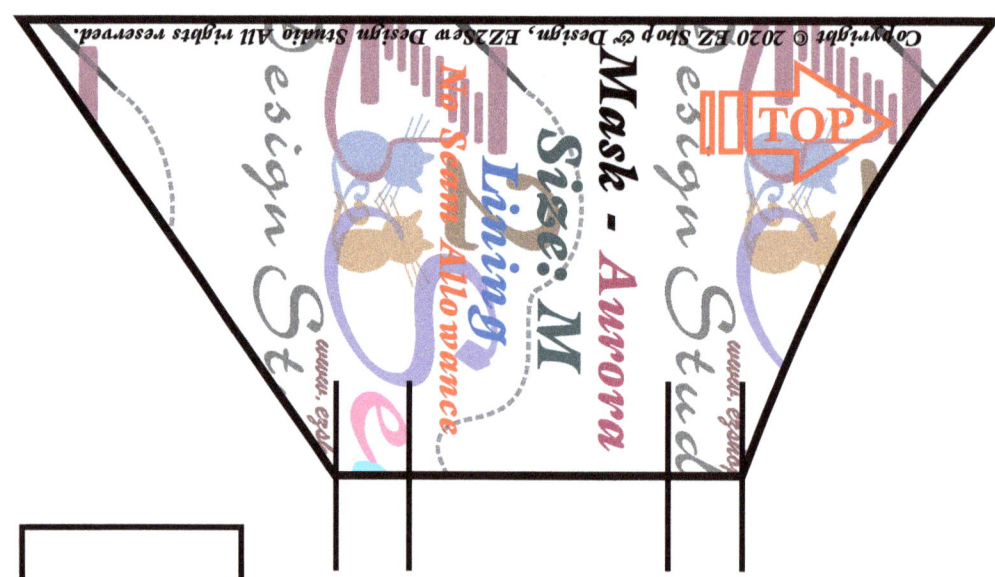

3cm

1"

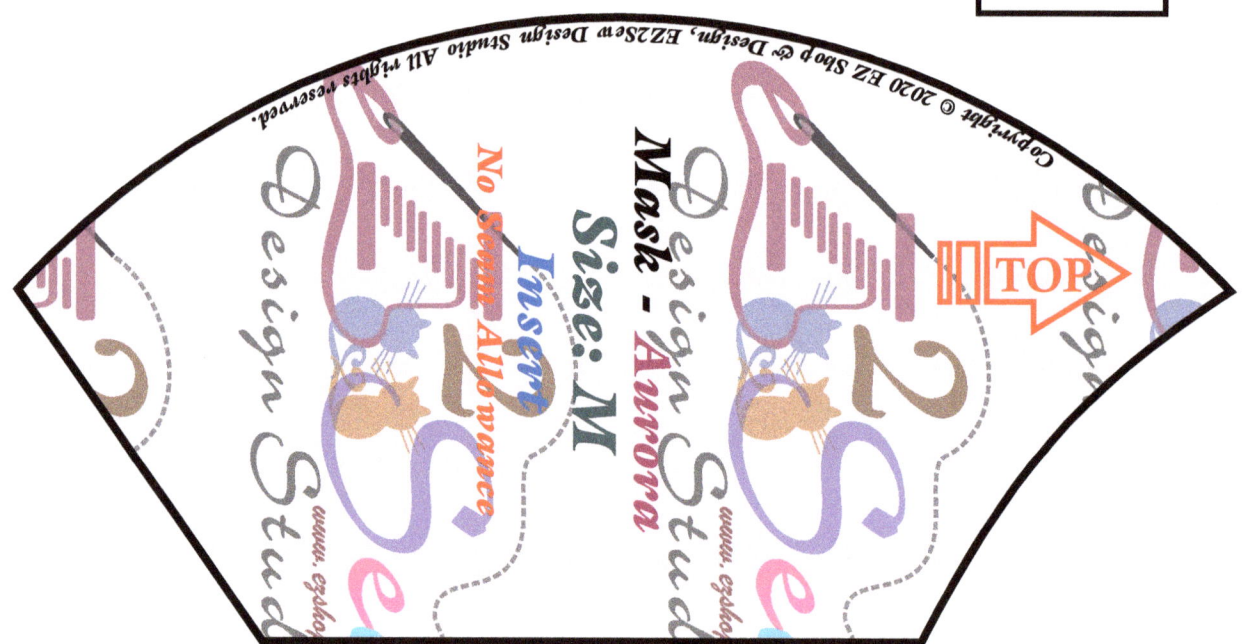

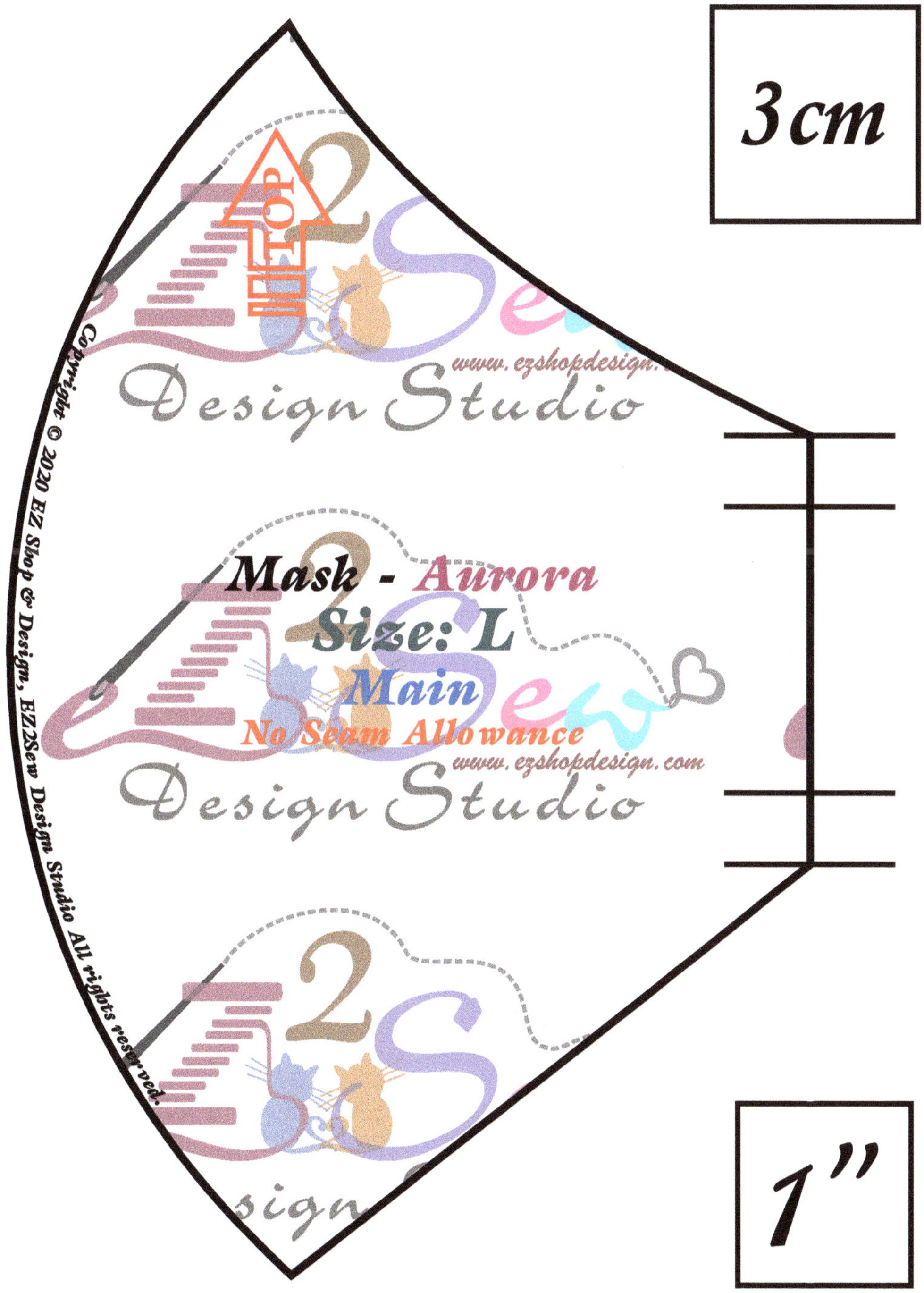

PATTERN

3cm

Mask - Aurora
Size: L
Main
No Seam Allowance

1"

Mask: Aurora

50

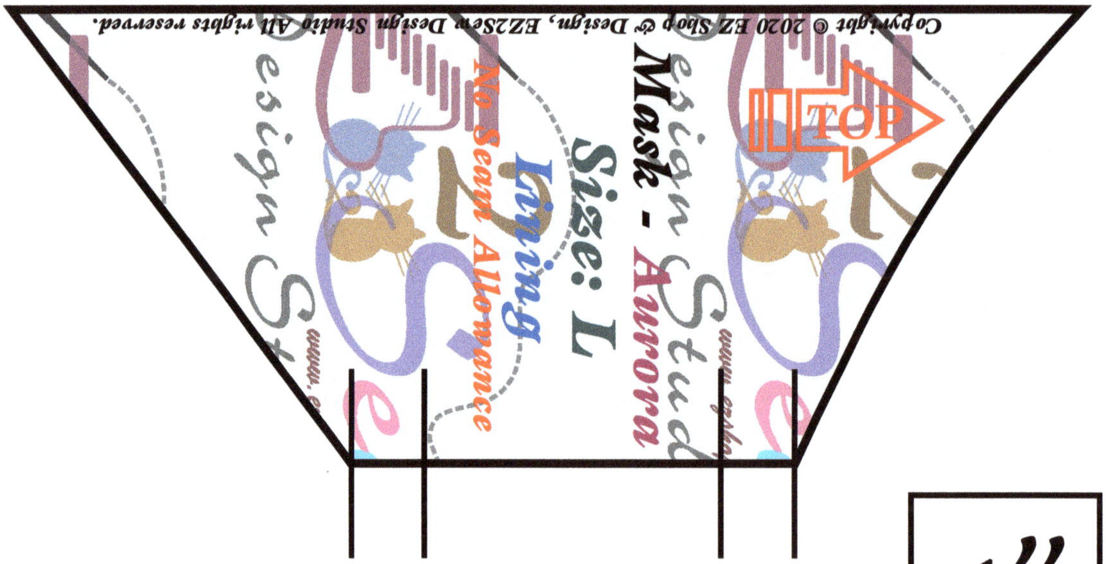

PATTERN

Mask: Aurora

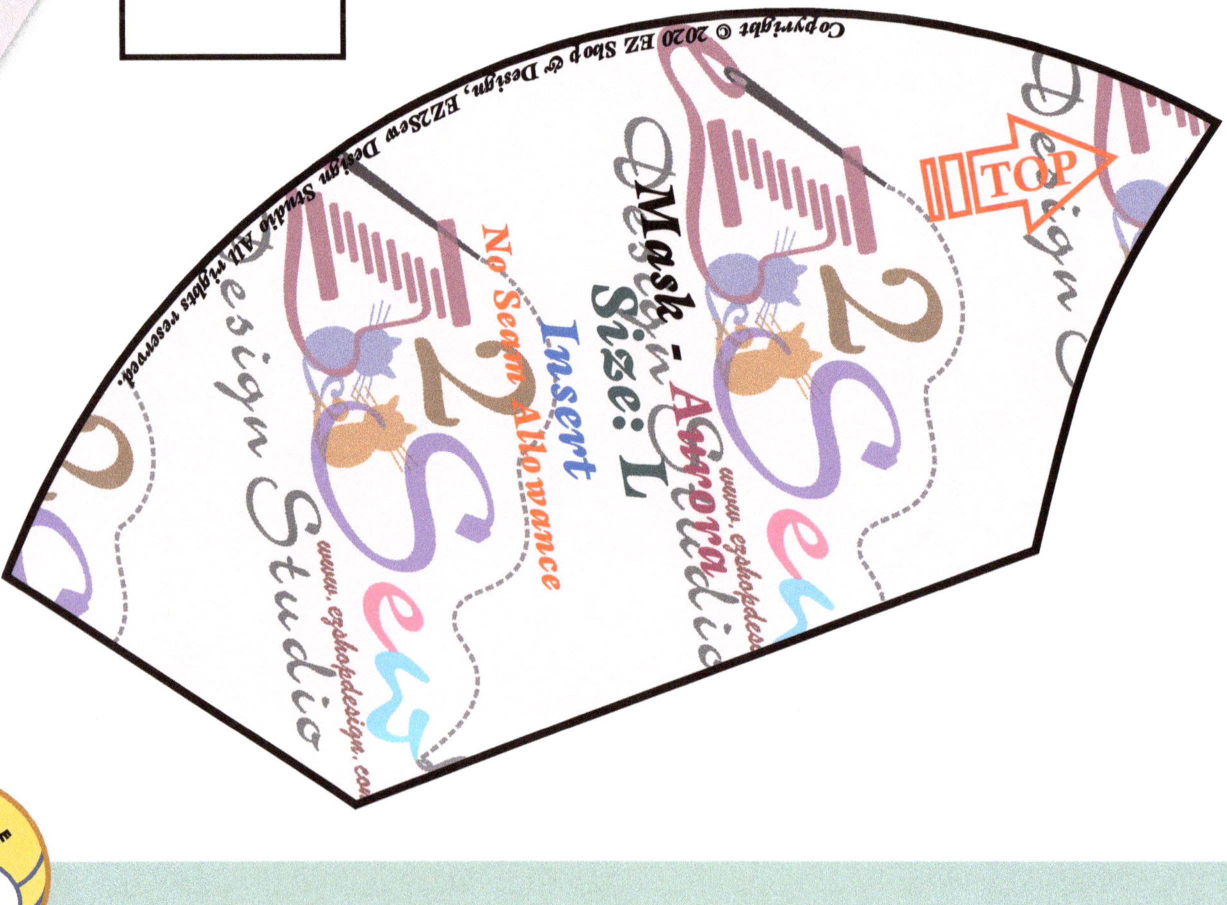

3cm

1"

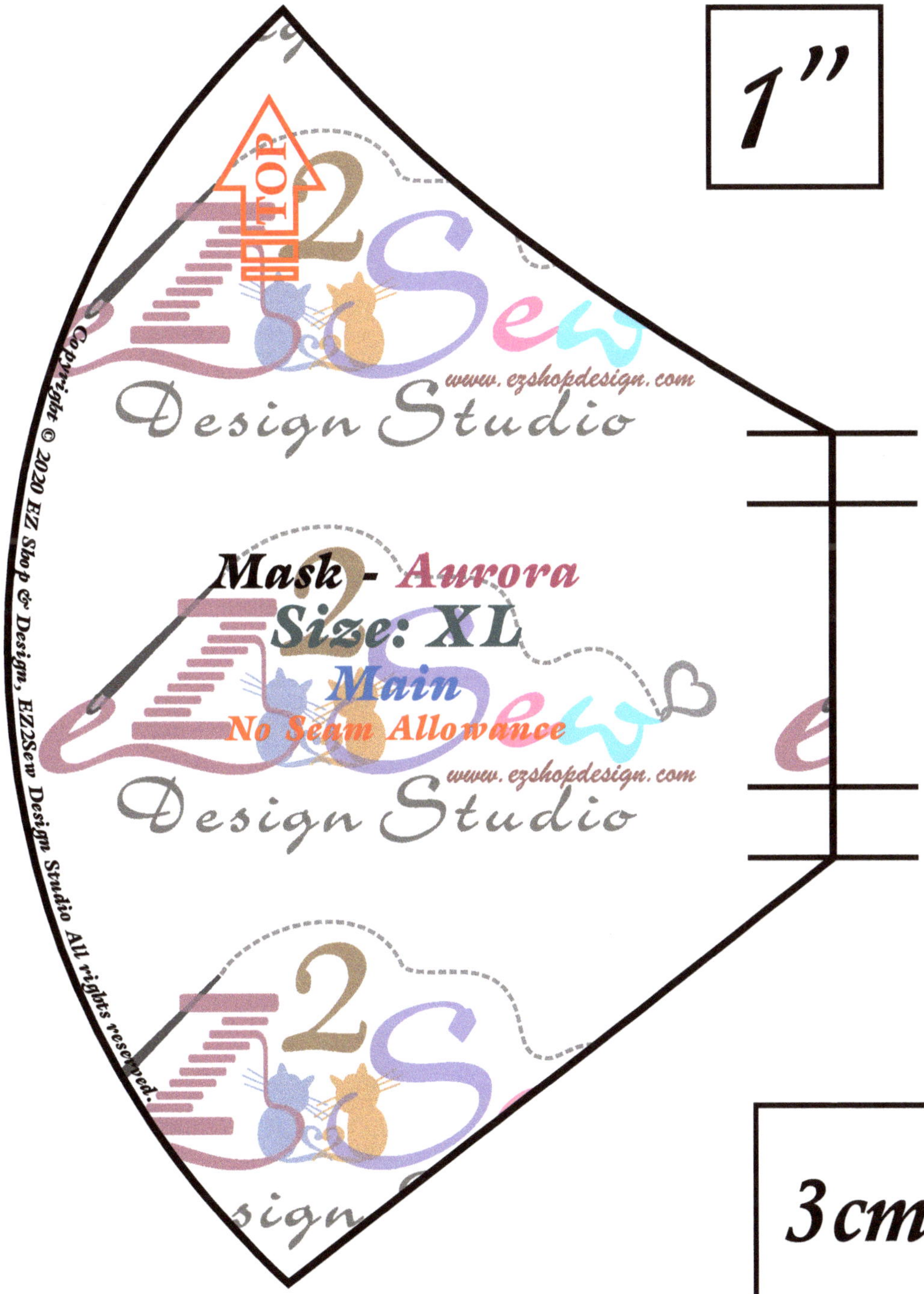

PATTERN

Mask: Aurora

1"

Mask - Aurora
Size: XL
Main
No Seam Allowance

3cm

52

PATTERN

Mask: Aurora

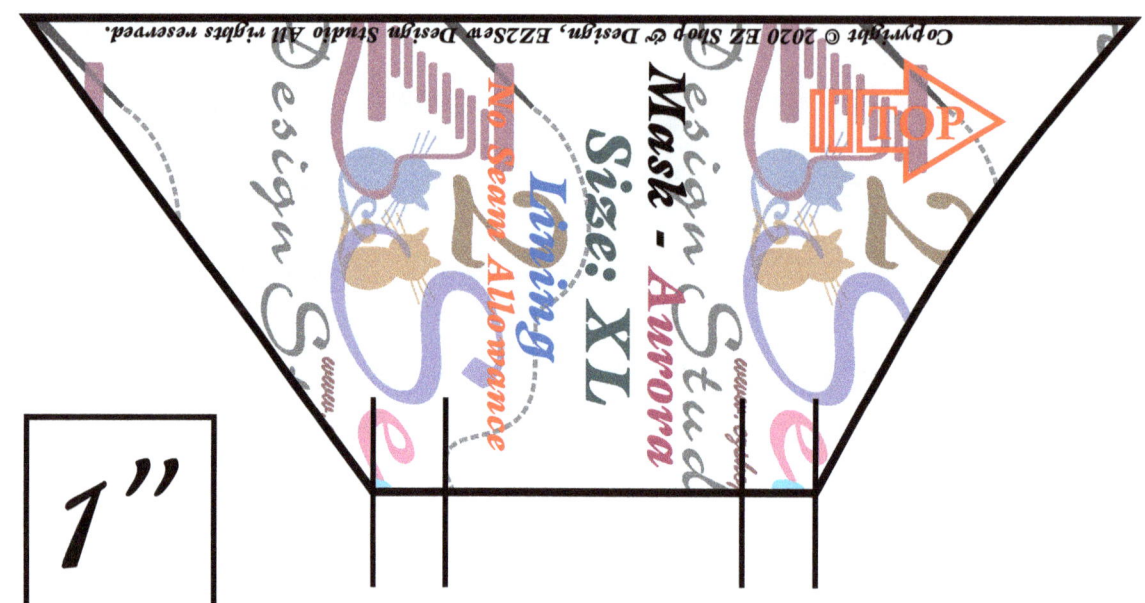

1"

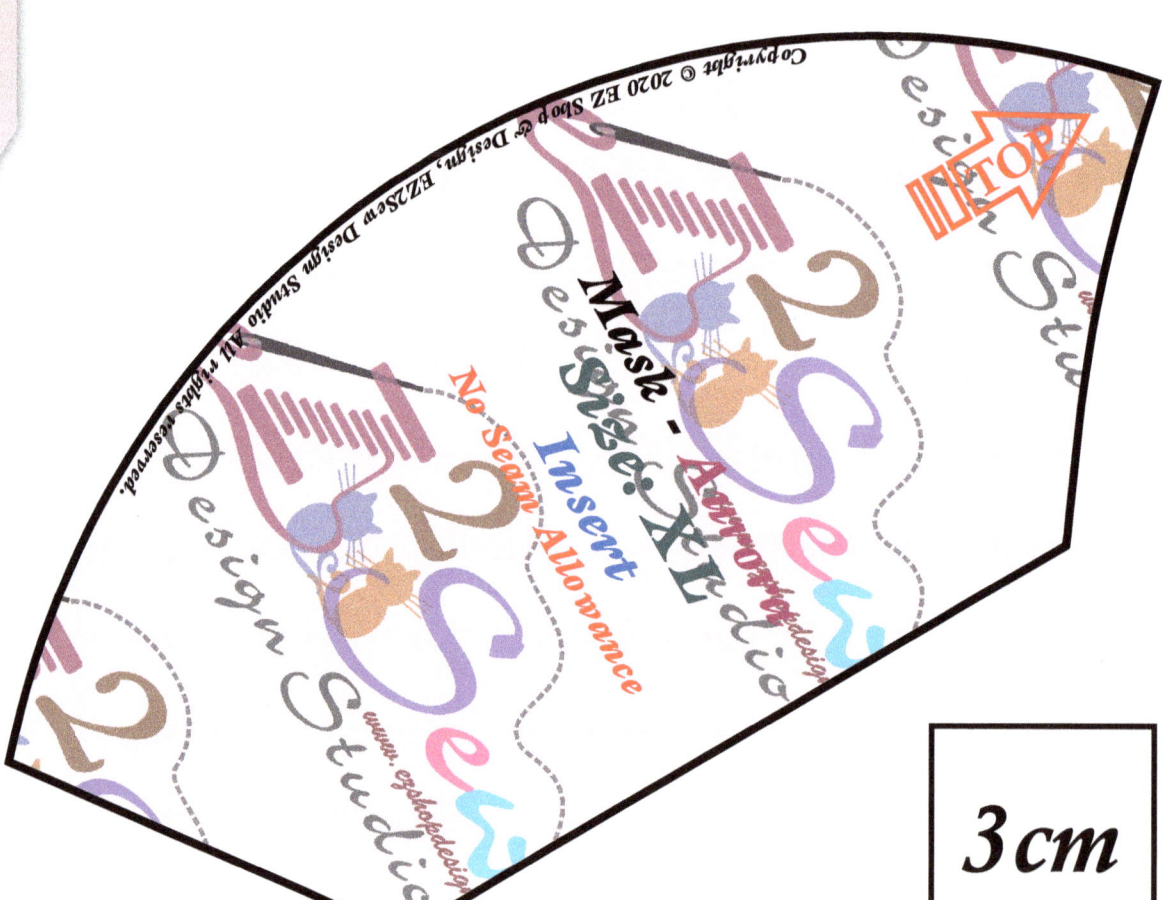

3cm

 # PATTERN

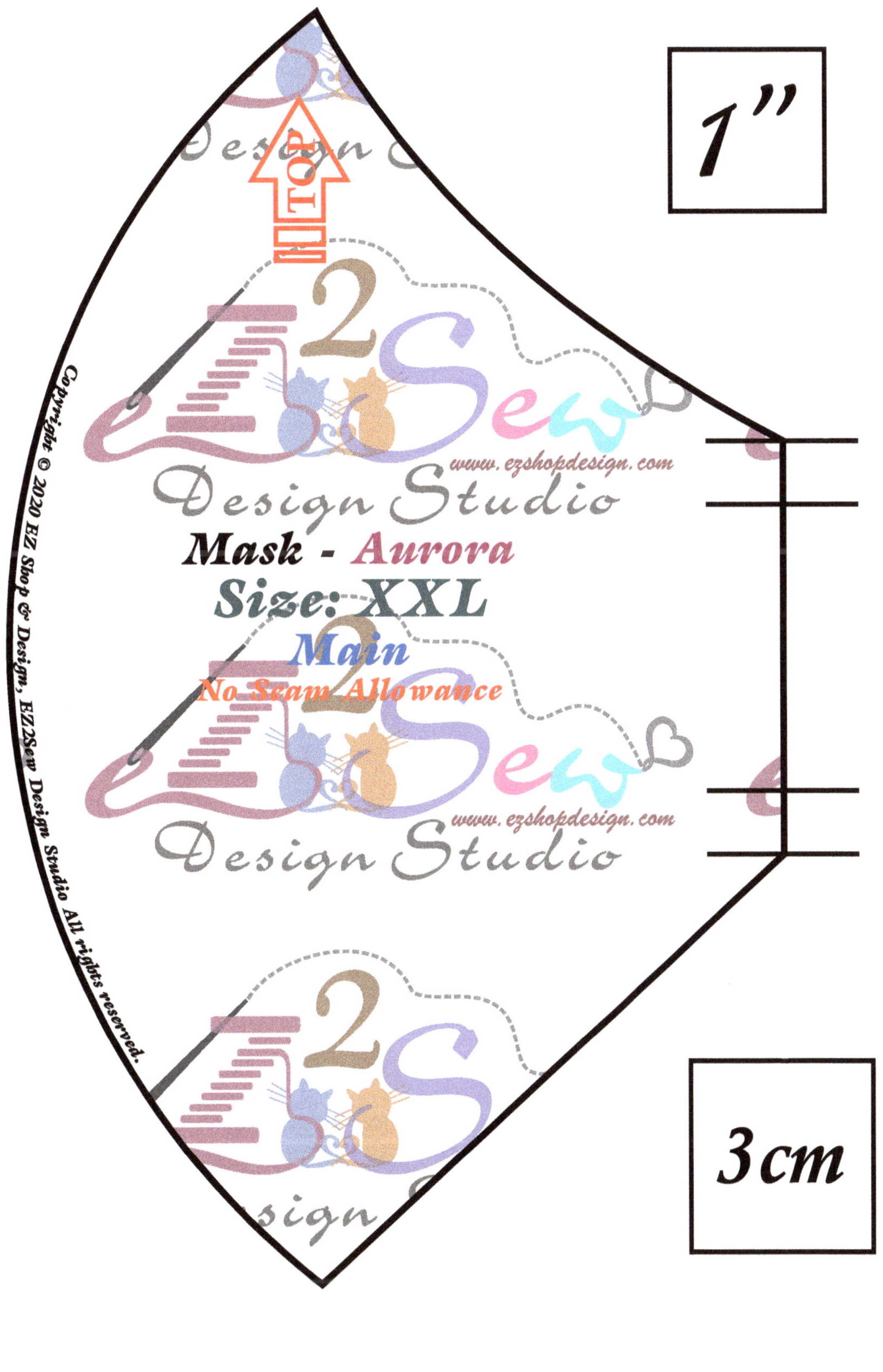

Mask: Aurora

1"

Mask - Aurora
Size: XXL
Main
No Seam Allowance

3cm

PATTERN

Mask: Aurora

1"

3cm

Mask - *Aurora*
Size: **XXL**
Insert
No Seam Allowance

Copyright © 2020 EZ Shop & Design, EZ2Sew Design Studio ALL rights reserved.

55

PATTERN

Mask: Aurora

Mask - Aurora
Size: XXL
Lining
No Seam Allowance

1"

3cm

56

BAYLEE

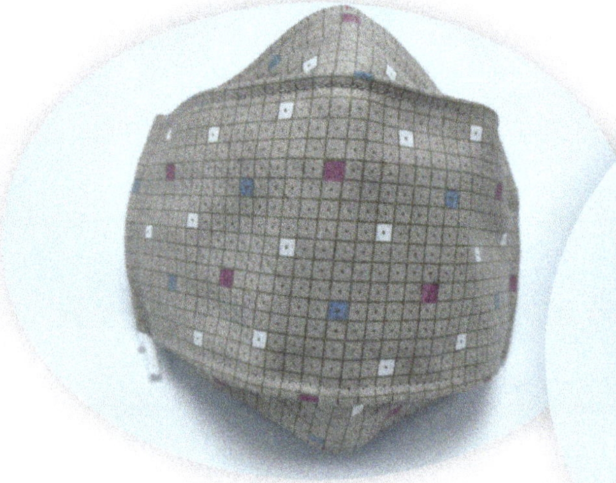

Mask: Baylee

PREPARATION

PREPARING ALL THE MATERIALS

✂ **For NON-Directional Fabrics**

Exterior/Interior:

- **Main** fabric - "Main" x 1;
- **Lining/Insert** fabric - "Lining/Insert" x 2;

🔧 **HARDWARE & ACCESSORY:** 10cm (3.9") Nose Wire Strip x 1; 20cm x 0.5cm (8" L x 0.2" W) Elastic x 2.

✂ **For Directional Fabrics**

- The same as non-directional fabrics; Make sure they are in the correct direction, especially the "Lining/Insert" piece.

✍ **NOTE:** Add seam allowance of your choice before cutting any fabric. No interfacing needed for making "Baylee" mask.

Construct the "Baylee" Mask

1 **Sew the Lining/Insert raw edge.** Double fold the flat edge of the "Lining/Insert" piece to the Wrong side, the same width as the seam allowance and sew to hide the raw edge. Do the same on the other "Lining/Insert" piece.

2 **Connect "Main" and "Lining/Insert" pieces.** Place one of the "Lining/Insert" pieces Wrong side facing up on top of the "Main" piece (Right side facing up), align the top centers. Place the other "Lining/Insert" piece Wrong side facing up, align the bottom centers. The overlapping area of both "Lining/Insert" pieces is in the middle.

DIRECTIONS

Construct the "Baylee" Mask

3. Sew. Sew ONLY the longer straight line at the top and bottom to connect both "Main" and "Lining/Insert" pieces, using the seam allowance of your choice.

4. Turn the piece Right side out. Flip both "Lining/Insert" pieces to the Right side, so that all three pieces will have the Wrong sides facing each other.

5. Topstitching. Top stitch both the top and bottom of the connected piece, using 3mm (1/8") seam allowance (Please refer to the photo).

6. (Optional) Make a casing. Mark 5cm away from the top center, sew to create a casing. Insert the Nose Wire Strip from the Wrong side.

7. Fold both top and bottom trapezoids to the center. Top Stitch both top and bottom folded edges, using 3mm (1/8") seam allowance.

8. Fold each corner of the trapezoid parallel to the side raw edge. Use clips to hold the corners in place (Please refer to the photo).

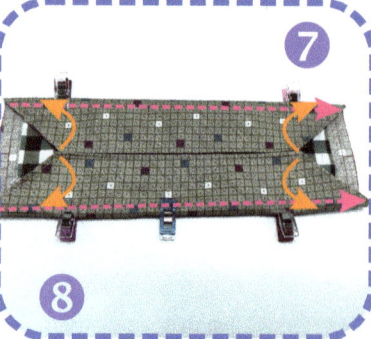

DIRECTIONS

Construct the "Baylee" Mask

9 **Make a elastic casing.** Fold the seam allowance of both raw edges towards the lining. Then fold again with a width of 1.5cm (0.6") to cover the corner you clipped down in step 8. Sew to create a casing to insert the elastic. Feed the elastic through the casing and tie a knot.

insert the elastic

Special Marking on the pattern

 The **diamond** shape marking indicates where you join/connect the pattern pieces together.

Figure 1

★ **Half diamond** (Figure 1):

❶ Print 2 copies of the same pattern piece.

❷ Cut out both copies and turn one of the pattern pieces to the reverse side (Figure 2).

❸ Line up both pieces to form the diamond.

❹ Use clear tape to connect both pieces together.

❺ The new pattern will be Pattern A (Figure 3) which has NO seam allowance. Add seam allowance of your choice all the way around to make the Pattern B before cutting any fabric.

Figure 2

 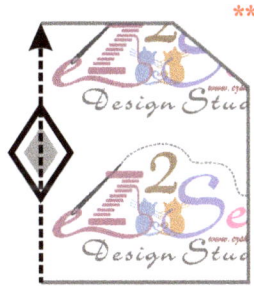

*** NOT an actual size of the pattern. Do NOT use it for cutting the fabric. ***

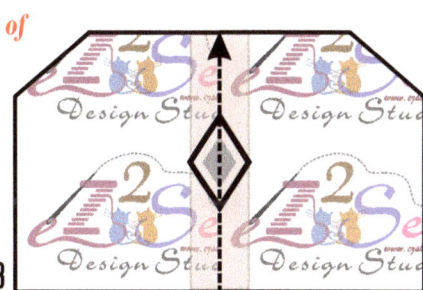

Figure 3

PATTERN

[Pattern]: Baylee

✦ **NOTE:** The attached pattern has <u>NO</u> seam allowances included. Add seam allowance of your choice (1/8", 1/4", 1/2" or 0.7 cm, 1 cm, 1.25 cm) before cutting any fabric or sewing! ☺

Figure 1

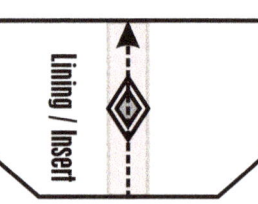

✦ **NOTE:** If you use **directional fabric**, please check **Figure 1** before cutting the "Lining/Insert" pieces.

3cm

1"

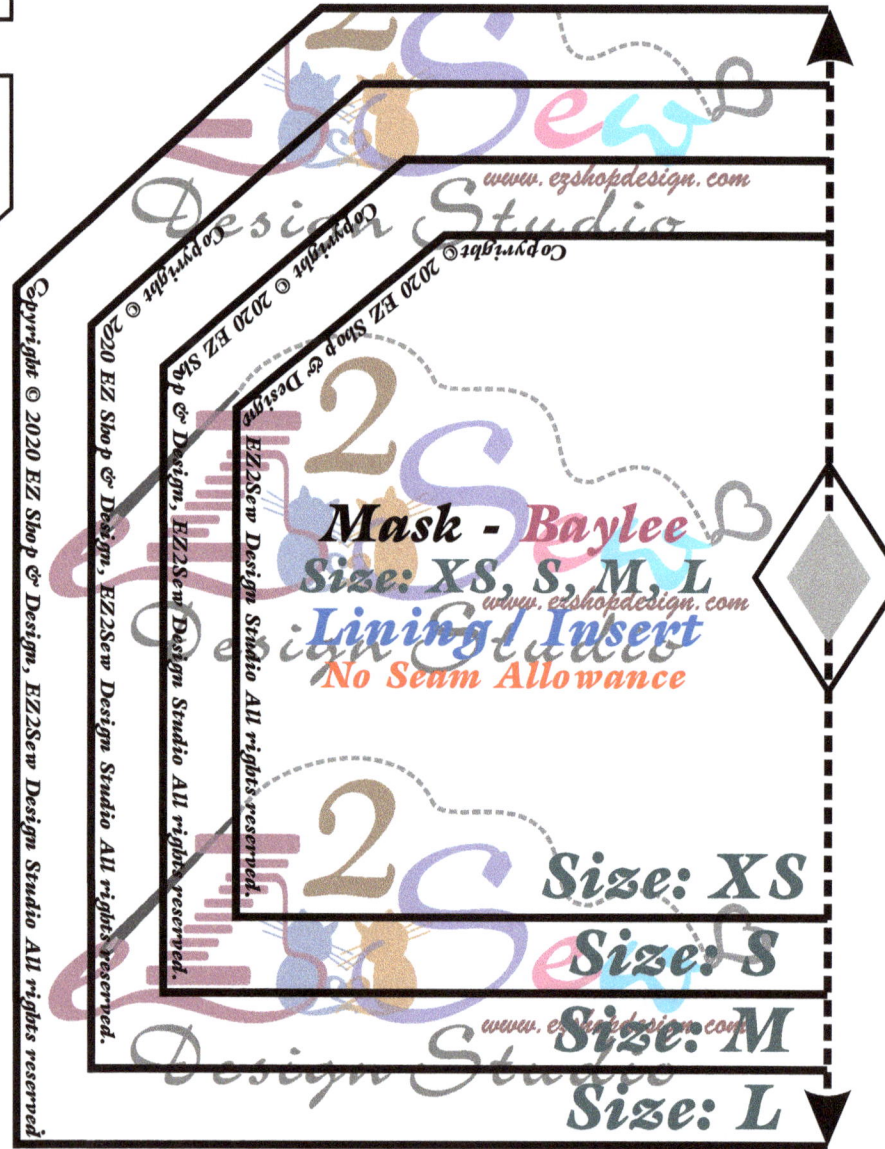

Mask - Baylee
Size: XS, S, M, L
Lining / Insert
No Seam Allowance

Size: XS
Size: S
Size: M
Size: L

PATTERN

1"

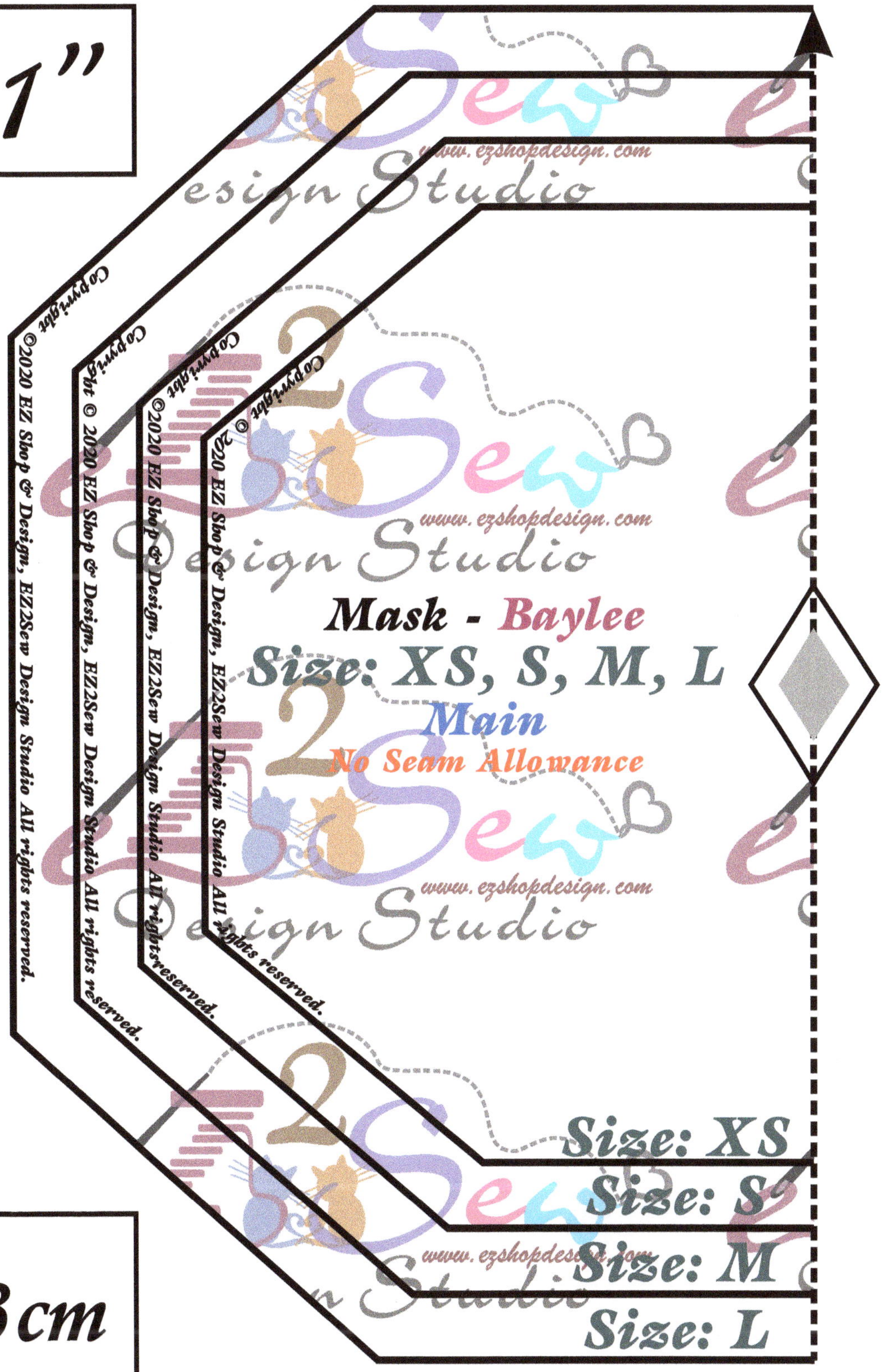

Mask - Baylee
Size: XS, S, M, L
Main
No Seam Allowance

Size: XS
Size: S
Size: M
Size: L

3cm

Mask: Baylee

62

BLOSSOM

Mask: Blossom

PREPARATION

PREPARING ALL THE MATERIALS

✂ For NON-Directional Fabrics

Exterior/Interior:

- **Main** fabric - "Main" x 1;
- **Lining** fabric - "Lining" x 2;
- **Insert** fabric - "Insert" x 1;

🛠 **HARDWARE & ACCESSORY:** (Optional) 10cm (3.9") Nose Wire Strip x 1; 0.5cm (0.2" W) Elastic x 1, Cord buckle (lock) x 1.

✂ For Directional Fabrics

- The same as non-directional fabrics; Make sure they are in the correct direction.

✍ **NOTE:** Add seam allowance of your choice before cutting any fabric. No interfacing needed for making "Blossom" mask.

Main

Insert

Lining

Reference

- ★ **Pattern A** - the original pattern which has "NO Seam Allowance"
- ★ **Pattern B** - add "Seam Allowance" of your choice (1/4", 3/8" or 1/2") to Pattern A

Mask: Blossom

DIRECTIONS

Construct the "Blossom" Mask

1 **Sew the Lining raw edge.** Double fold the taller straight side of the "Lining" piece to the Wrong side, the same width as the seam allowance and sew to hide the raw edge. Do the same on the other "Lining" piece.

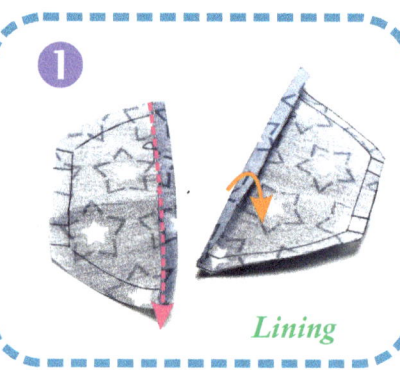
Lining

2 **Sew the Insert raw edge.** Double fold both straight sides of the "Insert" piece to the Wrong side, the same width as the seam allowance and sew to hide the raw edge.

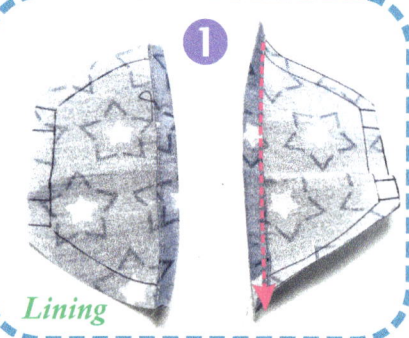
Lining

3 **Connect both "Main" and "Insert" pieces together.** Place the "Main" piece Right side up, then put the "Insert" piece on top of the "Main" piece, Right side facing down, align both centers. Use clips or pins to hold them in place.

Insert

4 **Connect all pieces together.** Place the "Lining" piece on each side of the "Insert" piece, Right side facing the Right side of the "Main" piece, align the markings on both shorter ends. (please refer to the photo and pattern).

Main *Insert*

Insert

Lining Insert Lining

DIRECTIONS

Construct the "Blossom" Mask

5 **Sew all the way around and leave 4 openings.** Sew all the way around using the seam allowance of your choice and leave four openings at corners. Don't forget to back stitches at each beginning and end (please refer to the photo and pattern markings).

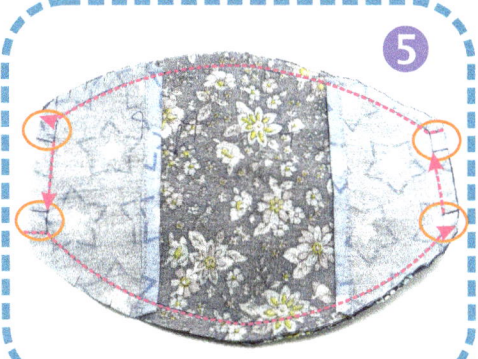

6 **Turn Right side out.** Make a few clips on the curved seam. Turn the whole piece Right side out through the opening between "Lining" and "Insert" pieces. Use your finger tip or something pointy (but not sharp) to round out the curved seam and four openings at corners.

7 **Top stitch.** Top stitch all the way around, except those four openings at corners, using 3mm (1/8") seam allowance (please refer to the photo above).

DIRECTIONS

Construct the "Blossom" Mask

8 **Make a casing.** Sew a casing about 1cm (3/8") wide away from the top stitched seam at both the top and bottom, leave a 1cm (3/8") opening before reaching the end (please refer to the photo).

9 **Feed the elastic cord through the openings.** Use the bodkin to feed the elastic cord through the casing all the way around. Cinch the elastic cord and gather the fabric to the center. Feed one of the elastic cord ends through the opposite opening at the same side and do the same as the other end. Tie a knot from the inside of the "Lining" or use a cord buckle/lock (please refer to the photos).

Optional: Insert a nose strip (if needed) through the "Insert" casing

PATTERN

[Pattern]: Blossom

✮ ***NOTE:*** The attached pattern has **NO** seam allowances included. Add seam allowance of your choice (1/8", 1/4", 1/2" or 0.7 cm, 1 cm, 1.25 cm) before cutting any fabric or sewing! ☺

✮ ***NOTE:*** Fold the fabric in half, Right side facing together, add seam allowances all the way around the "***Lining***" pattern, and then cut 2 pieces. Please make sure the fabric is in correct direction before cutting.

Mask: Blossom

3 cm

1"

Printing Instructions

𝒫lease make sure your printer's scaling is set to "none," "actual size" or "100%". Do NOT check the "scale to fit paper size" option. Once the pattern is printed out, make sure it printed correctly. Check the "1 inch (3 cm) Square" and it should measure 1" x 1" (3 cm x 3 cm). If the square is not the correct size, check the printer settings again.

Mask - Blossom
Size: XS~L
Lining
No Seam Allowance

XS
S
M
L

PATTERN

Mask: Blossom

3cm

Mask - Blossom
Size: XS~L
Insert
No Seam Allowance

XS
S
M
L

1"

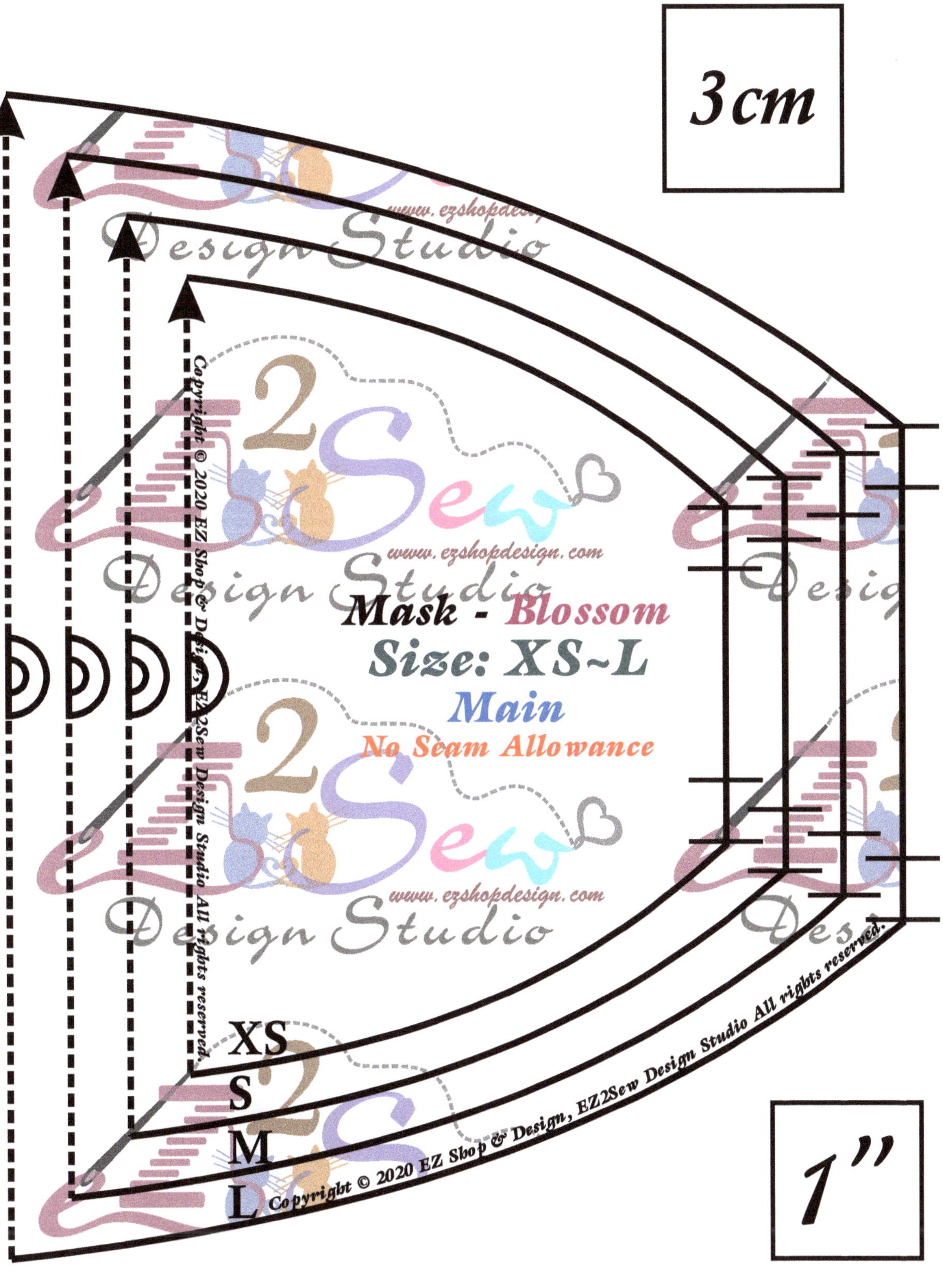

PATTERN

Mask: Blossom

3cm

Mask - Blossom
Size: XS~L
Main
No Seam Allowance

XS
S
M
L

1"

LYDIA

Mask: Lydia

PREPARATION

PREPARING ALL THE MATERIALS

✂ **For NON-Directional Fabrics**

Exterior/Interior:

- **Main** fabric - "Main" x 1;
- **Lining** fabric - "Lining" x 2;

🔧 **HARDWARE & ACCESSORY:** 10cm (3.9") Nose Wire Strip x 1; 20cm x 0.5cm (8" L x 3/16" W) Elastic x 2, (Optional) 8cm x 0.5cm (3.15" L x 3/16" W) Elastic x 1; (Optional) Cord buckle/lock x 2.

✂ **For Directional Fabrics**

- The same as non-directional fabrics; Make sure they are in the correct direction.

✏ **NOTE:** Add seam allowance of your choice before cutting any fabric. No interfacing needed for making "Lydia" mask.

Construct the "Lydia" Mask

1 **Transfer all the markings to the fabric.** Add the seam allowance of your choice before cutting the fabric. Transfer all the markings from the pattern to the fabric (please refer to the photo).

2 **Connect both "Lining" pieces.** Place both "Lining" pieces Right sides facing each other, sew only the top and bottom seam allowance on the side with no markings (please refer to the photo).

3 **Sew to hide the raw edge of the connected "Lining" piece.** Double fold the seam allowance raw edges inward to the Wrong side. Sew to hide the raw edge. Do the same on the other side (please refer to the photo).

DIRECTIONS

Construct the "Lydia" Mask

4. **Sew the pleats.** Fold the pleats on the connected "Lining" piece either upward or downward (Please refer to the pattern markings) and sew to hold them in place. Do the same on the "Main" piece and fold the pleats in the same direction as you folded on the "Lining".

5. **Connect the "Main" and "Lining". Sew all the way around, except those 4 corners.** Place the "Main" piece Right side facing up and both "Lining" pieces Right side facing down, align right and left pleats. Sew all the way around using the seam allowance of your choice, but leave those openings at the 4 corners (Please refer to the photo).

6. **Turn Right side out and Top stitch.** Turn the whole piece Right side out through the "Lining" opening on the center. Top stitch the top, bottom and both sides using 3mm (1/8") seam allowance. Do NOT sew the openings at the four corners. Back stitch at all the beginnings and ends.

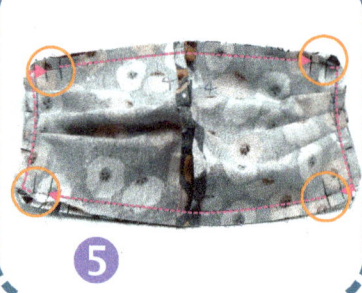

7. **Make a casing.** Mark 5cm away from the top center, create a casing to insert the Nose Wire Strip from the center opening of the "Lining" (please refer to the photo).

Feed the elastic through the bottom casing

☞ **[Optional]: Make a casing.** Mark 4.5cm away from the bottom center, create a casing to feed the 9cm elastic cord from inside of the "Lining", cinch the elastic down to the length you prefer (about 4~5cm). Use clips to hold both elastic ends and sew to close. Trim the excess elastic. Please refer to the photo.

DIRECTIONS

Construct the "Lydia" Mask

8 **Feed the elastic through the openings.** Feed the elastic through the corner opening and tie a knot from inside or use an elastic cord buckle/lock (please refer to the photos below).

Bend the wire strip in half
Feed through from the opening ⑦

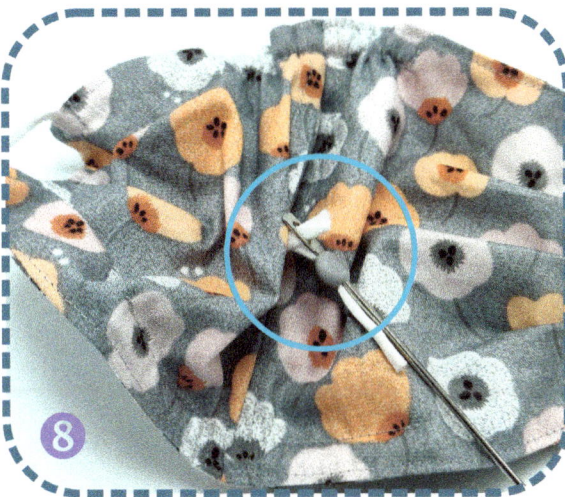

PATTERN

[Pattern]: Lydia

✦ **NOTE:** *The attached pattern has NO seam allowances included. Add seam allowance of your choice (1/8", 1/4", 1/2" or 0.7 cm, 1 cm, 1.25 cm) before cutting any fabric or sewing!* ☺

✦ **NOTE:** *For cutting the "**Main**" piece: Fold the fabric in half, Right side facing together. Align the double half circle marking to the folded fabric. Add seam allowances all the way around the pattern, and then cut 1 piece. Please make sure the fabric is in correct direction before cutting.*

1"

3cm

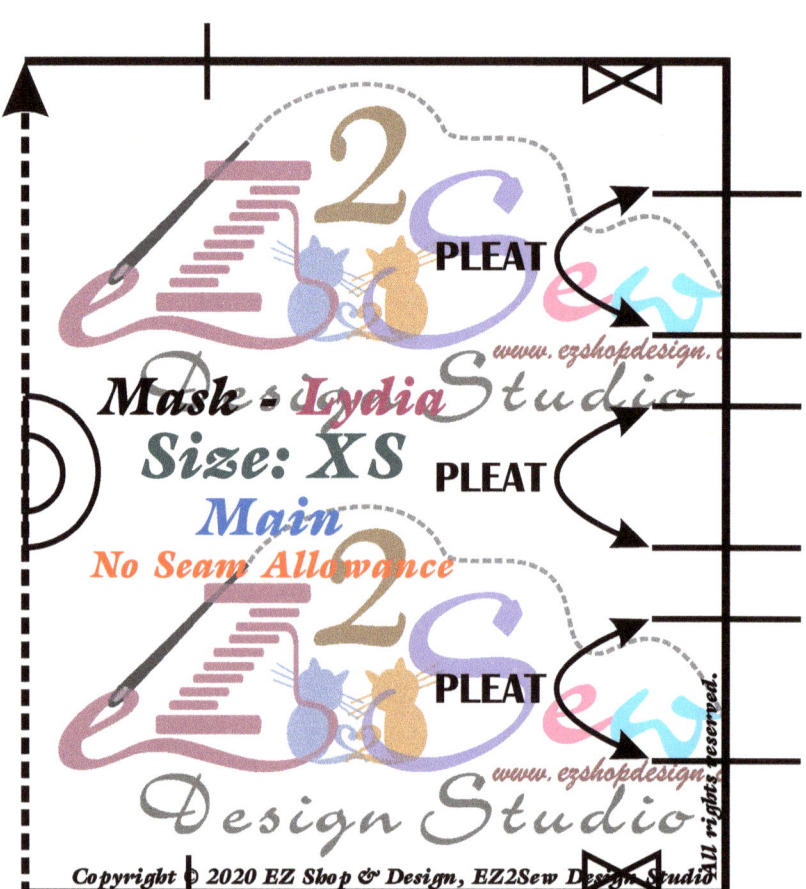

PATTERN

☆ **NOTE:** For cutting the "*Lining*" pieces: Add seam allowances all the way around the pattern, except one side (please refer to the pattern below), and then cut 2 pieces. Please make sure the fabric is in correct direction before cutting.

Printing Instructions

Please make sure your printer's scaling is set to "none," "actual size" or "100%". Do NOT check the "scale to fit paper size" option. Once the pattern is printed out, make sure it printed correctly. Check the "1 inch (3 cm) Square" and it should measure 1" x 1" (3 cm x 3 cm). If the square is not the correct size, check the printer settings again.

| 1" |
| 3 cm |

Mask: Lydia
Size: XS
Lining
No Seam Allowance

(NO seam allowance needed HERE)

PLEAT
PLEAT
PLEAT

www.ezshopdesign.com

Copyright © 2020 EZ Shop & Design, EZ2Sew Design Studio. All rights reserved.

PATTERN

Mask: Lydia

| 1" |

Mask - Lydia
Size: XS
Main
No Seam Allowance
PLEAT
PLEAT
PLEAT

Copyright © 2020 EZ Shop & Design, EZ2Sew Design Studio

| 3cm |

PATTERN

Mask: Lydia

1"

(NO seam allowance needed HERE)

Mask - Lydia
Size: S
Lining
No Seam Allowance

PLEAT
PLEAT
PLEAT

Copyright © 2020 EZ Shop & Design, EZ2Sew Design Studio. All rights reserved.

3cm

PATTERN

1"

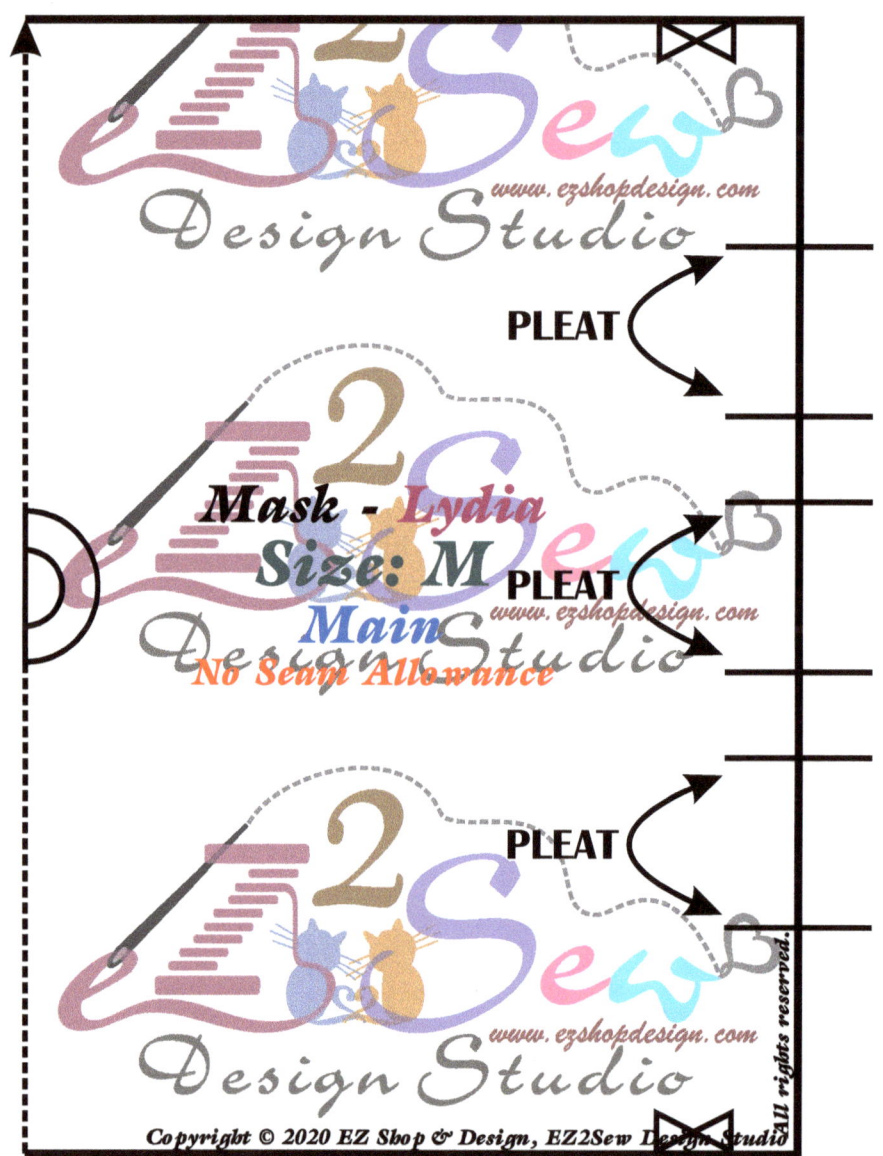

Mask - Lydia
Size: M
Main
No Seam Allowance

PLEAT
PLEAT
PLEAT

Copyright © 2020 EZ Shop & Design, EZ2Sew Design Studio. All rights reserved.

3cm

Mask: Lydia

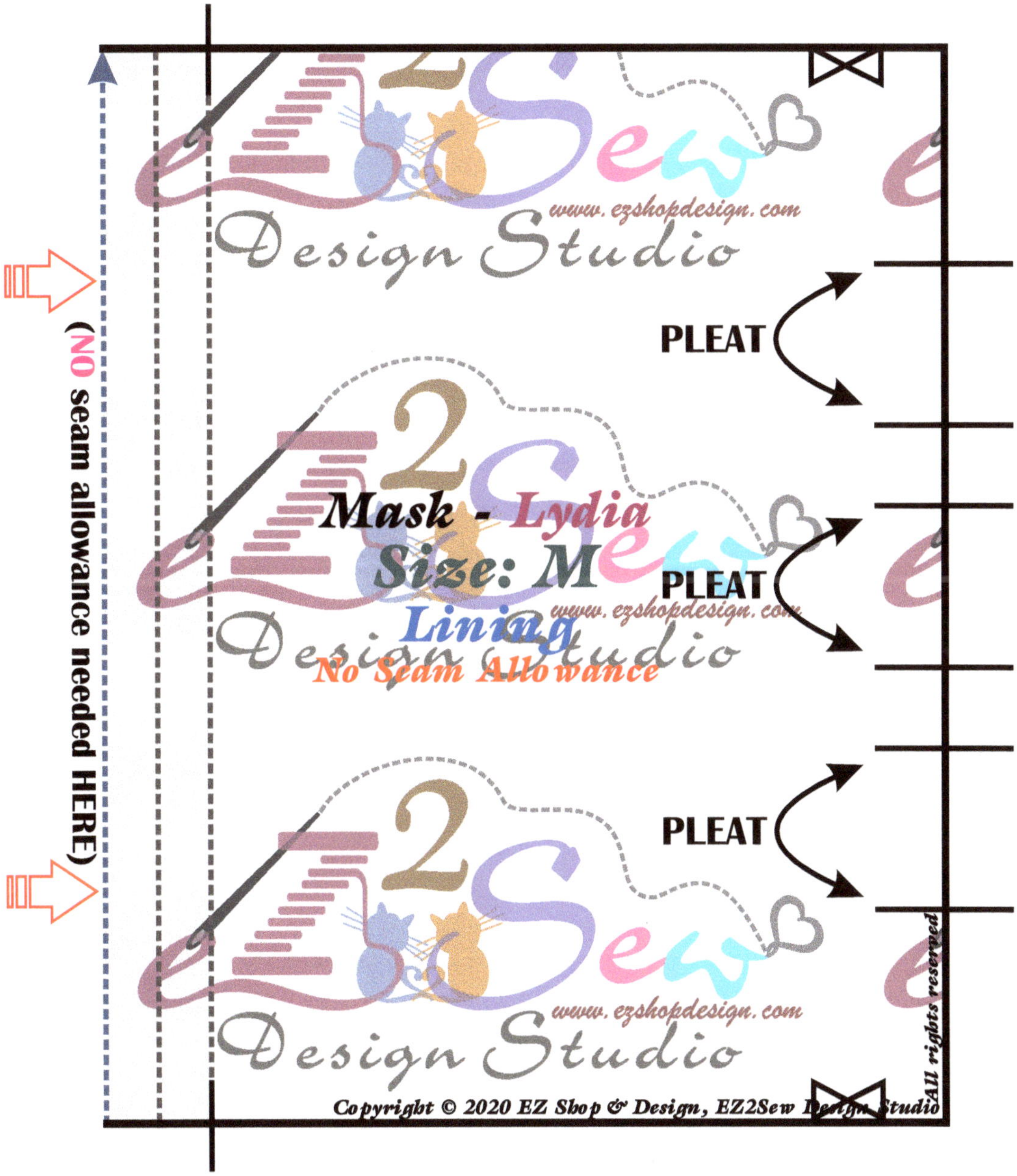

PATTERN

Mask: Lydia

(NO seam allowance needed HERE)

PLEAT

Mask - Lydia
Size: M
Lining
No Seam Allowance

PLEAT

PLEAT

1"

3cm

PATTERN

Mask: Lydia

Mask - Lydia
Size: L
Main
No Seam Allowance

PLEAT

PLEAT

PLEAT

3cm

1"

Copyright © 2020 EZ Shop & Design, EZ2Sew Design Studio. All rights reserved.

PATTERN

Mask: Lydia

Mask - Lydia
Size: L
Lining
No Seam Allowance

(NO seam allowance needed HERE)

PLEAT
PLEAT
PLEAT

Copyright © 2020 EZ Shop & Design, EZ2Sew Design Studio. All rights reserved.

1"

3cm

82

LUNA

Mask: Luna

PREPARATION

PREPARING ALL THE MATERIALS

✂ For NON-Directional Fabrics

Exterior/Interior:

- **Main** fabric - "Main" x 1;
- **Lining** fabric - "Lining" x 2;

🔧 **HARDWARE & ACCESSORY:** 10cm (3.9") Nose Wire Strip x 1; 20cm x 0.5cm (8" L x 3/16" W) Elastic x 2; (Optional) Cord buckle/lock x 2.

✂ For Directional Fabrics

- The same as non-directional fabrics; Make sure they are in the correct direction.

 NOTE: Add seam allowance of your choice before cutting any fabric (please check the pattern pages for more information). No interfacing needed for making "Luna" mask.

Construct the "Luna" Mask

1 Transfer all the markings to the fabric. Add the seam allowance of your choice before cutting fabric. Transfer all the markings from the pattern to the fabric (please refer to the photo).

2 Connect both "Lining" pieces. Place both "Lining" pieces Right sides facing each other, sew only the top and bottom seam allowance on the side without darts (Please refer to the photo).

3 Sew to hide the raw edge of the connected "Lining" piece. Double fold the seam allowance raw edges inward to the Wrong side. Sew to hide the raw edge. Do the same on the other side (please refer to the photo next page).

Mask: Luna

84

DIRECTIONS

Construct the "Luna" Mask

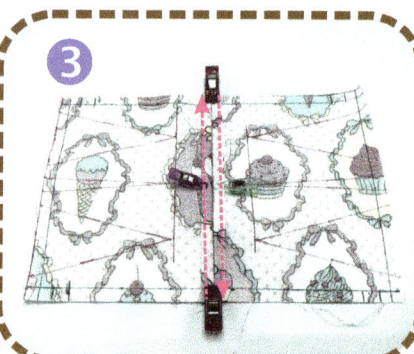

4 **Sew the darts.** Fold the longer sides of the "Main" piece, top and bottom, align to the center line. Sew all larger darts (2 on each side) on the marking. Cut the excess fabric of the darts and press the seam flat. Open the "Main" piece and fold it in half, sew the 2 small darts at the center and then press the seam flat (please refer to the photo).

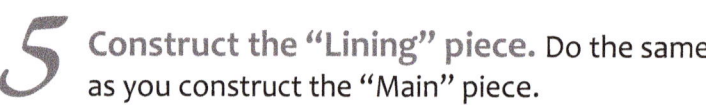

5 **Construct the "Lining" piece.** Do the same as you construct the "Main" piece.

6 **Connect "Main" and "Lining".** Sew all the way around, except those 4 corners.
Place both pieces Right side facing each other, align centers and folded darts. Sew all the way around using the seam allowance of your choice, but leave 4 openings at the corners (Please refer to the photo).

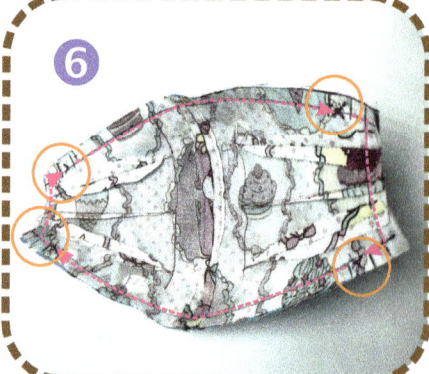

DIRECTIONS

Construct the "Luna" Mask

7 **Turn Right side out and Top stitch.** Turn the whole piece Right side out through the "Lining" center opening. Top stitch the top, bottom and both sides using 3mm (1/8") seam allowance. Do NOT sew close those 4 openings at the corners.

8 **Make a casing.** Mark 5cm away from the top center, create a casing to feed the Nose Wire Strip through the Center of the "Lining" opening (please refer to the photo).

9 **Feed the elastic through those 4 openings.** Feed the elastic through the corner openings and tie a knot from inside or use an elastic cord buckle/lock.

Bend the wire strip in half

Feed through from the opening

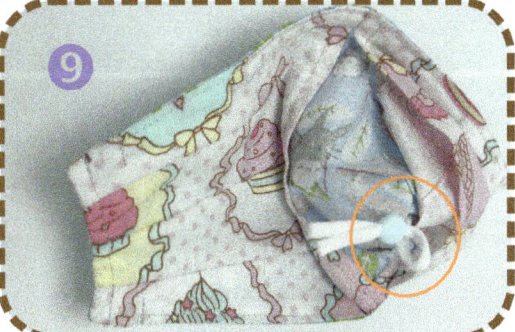

PATTERN

[Pattern]: Luna

☆ **NOTE:** The attached pattern has <u>NO</u> seam allowances included. Add seam allowance of your choice (1/8", 1/4", 1/2" or 0.7 cm, 1 cm, 1.25 cm) before cutting any fabric or sewing! ☺

☆ **NOTE:** For cutting the "**Main**" piece: Fold the fabric in half, Right side facing together. Align the double half circle marking to the folded fabric. Add seam allowances all the way around the pattern, and then cut 1 piece. Please make sure the fabric is in correct direction before cutting. *Do NOT cut the darts open and NO need to add seam allowance around the darts.*

1"

3cm

PATTERN

Mask: Luna

★ **NOTE:** For cutting the "**Lining**" pieces: Add seam allowances all the way around the pattern, except one side (please refer to the pattern below), and then cut 2 pieces. Please make sure the fabric is in correct direction before cutting. **Do NOT cut the darts open and NO need to add seam allowance around the darts.**

Printing Instructions

Please make sure your printer's scaling is set to "none," "actual size" or "100%". Do NOT check the "scale to fit paper size" option. Once the pattern is printed out, make sure it printed correctly. Check the "1 inch (3 cm) Square" and it should measure 1" x 1" (3 cm x 3 cm). If the square is not the correct size, check the printer settings again.

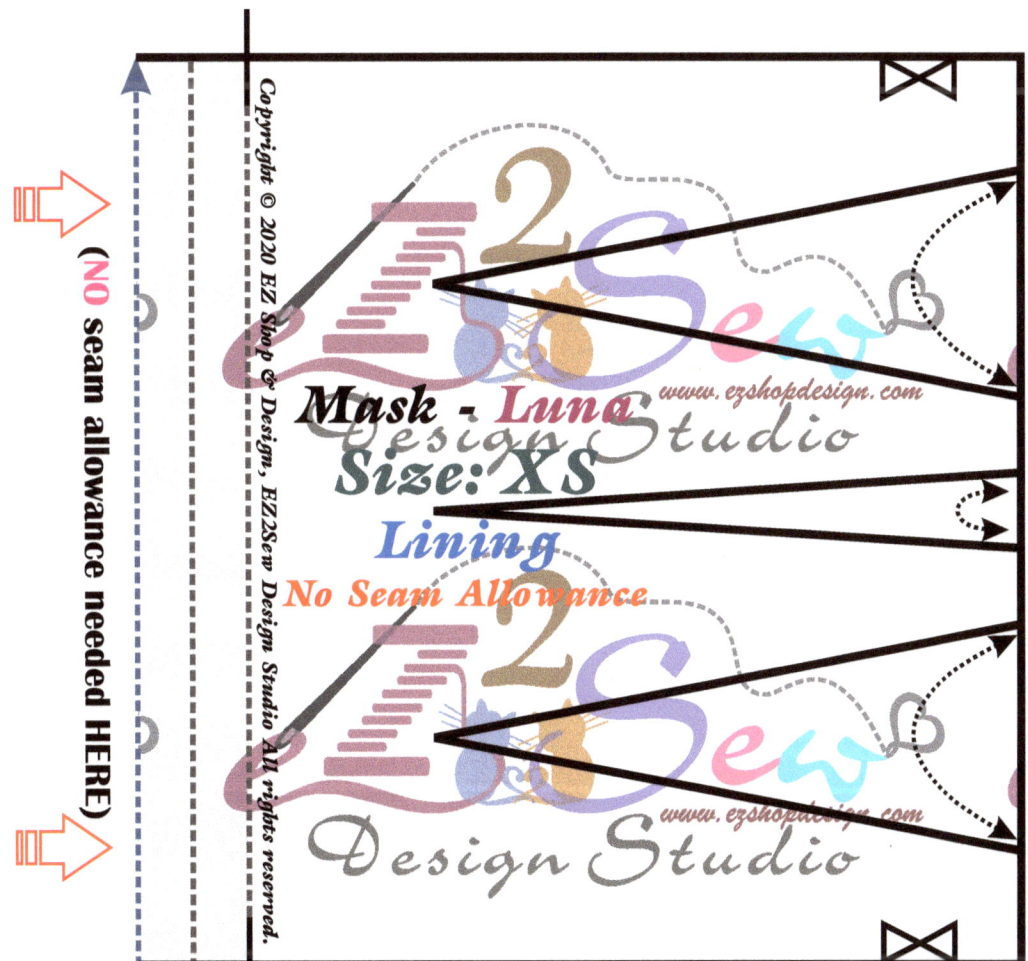

Mask - Luna
Size: XS
Lining
No Seam Allowance
(NO seam allowance needed HERE)

PATTERN

Mask: Luna

Mask - Luna
Size: S
Main
No Seam Allowance

| 1" | 3cm |

PATTERN

| 1" | 3cm |

Mask: Luna

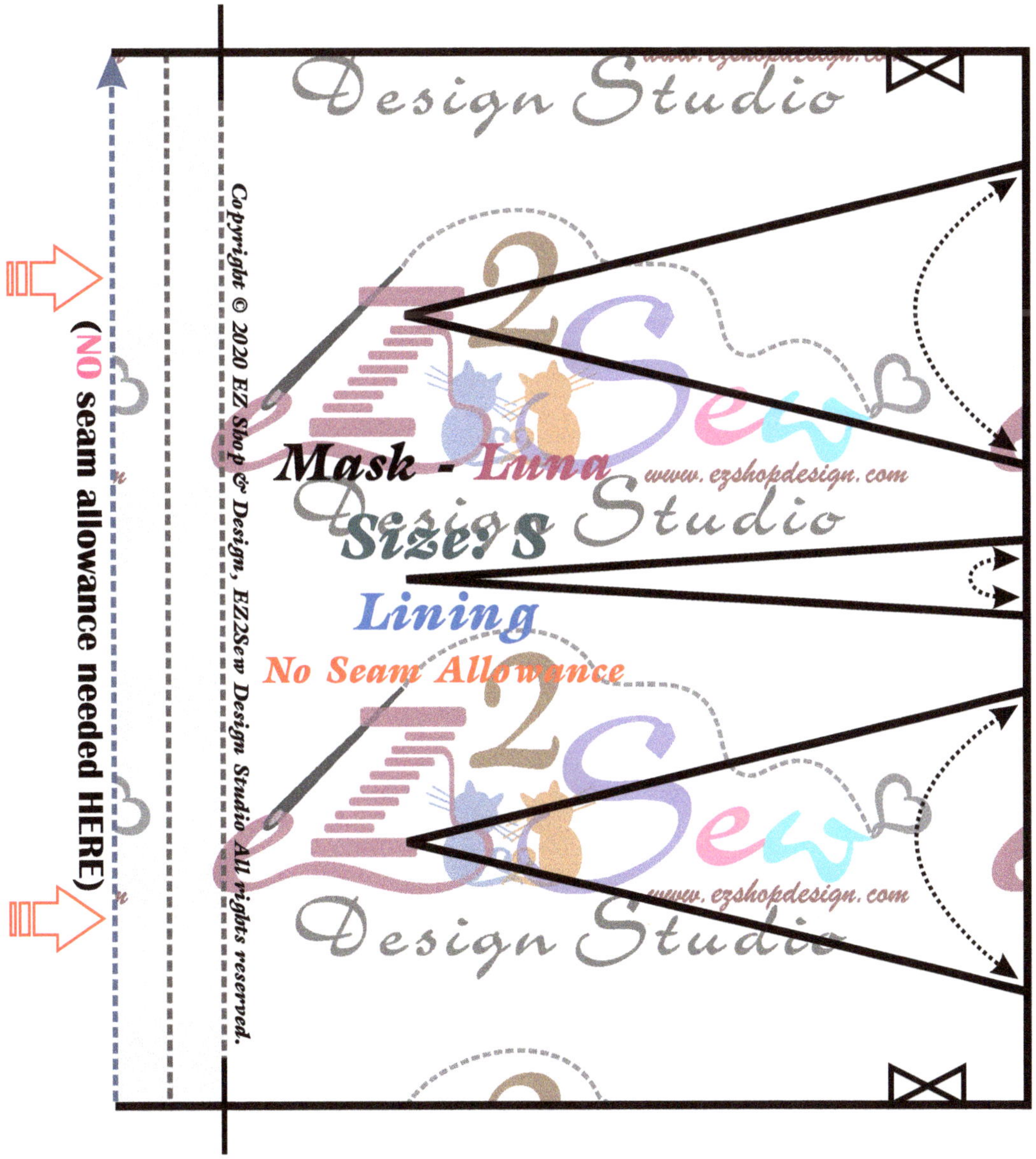

Mask - Luna
Size: S
Lining
No Seam Allowance

(NO seam allowance needed HERE)

90

PATTERN

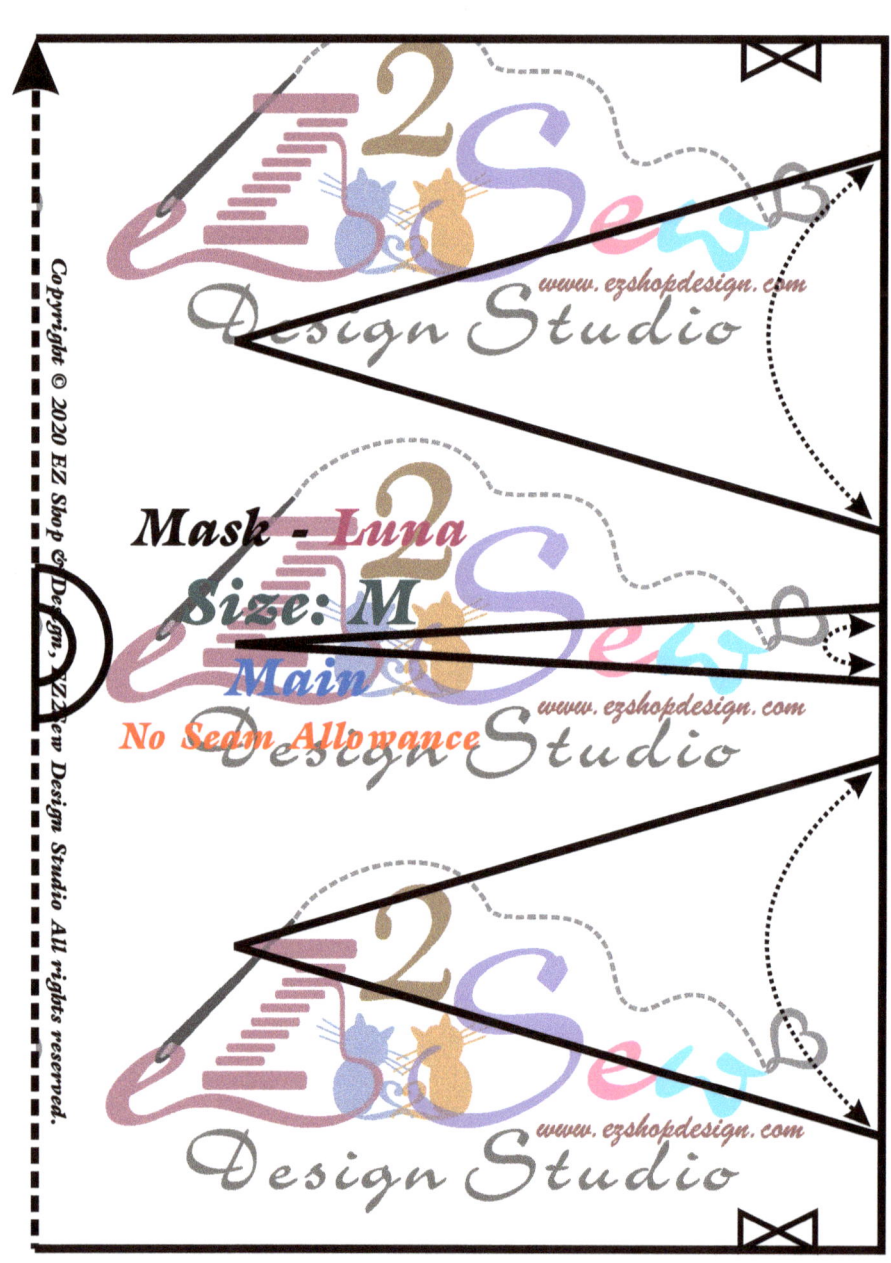

Mask - Luna
Size: M
Main
No Seam Allowance

1"   3cm

PATTERN

1" 3cm

Mask: Luna

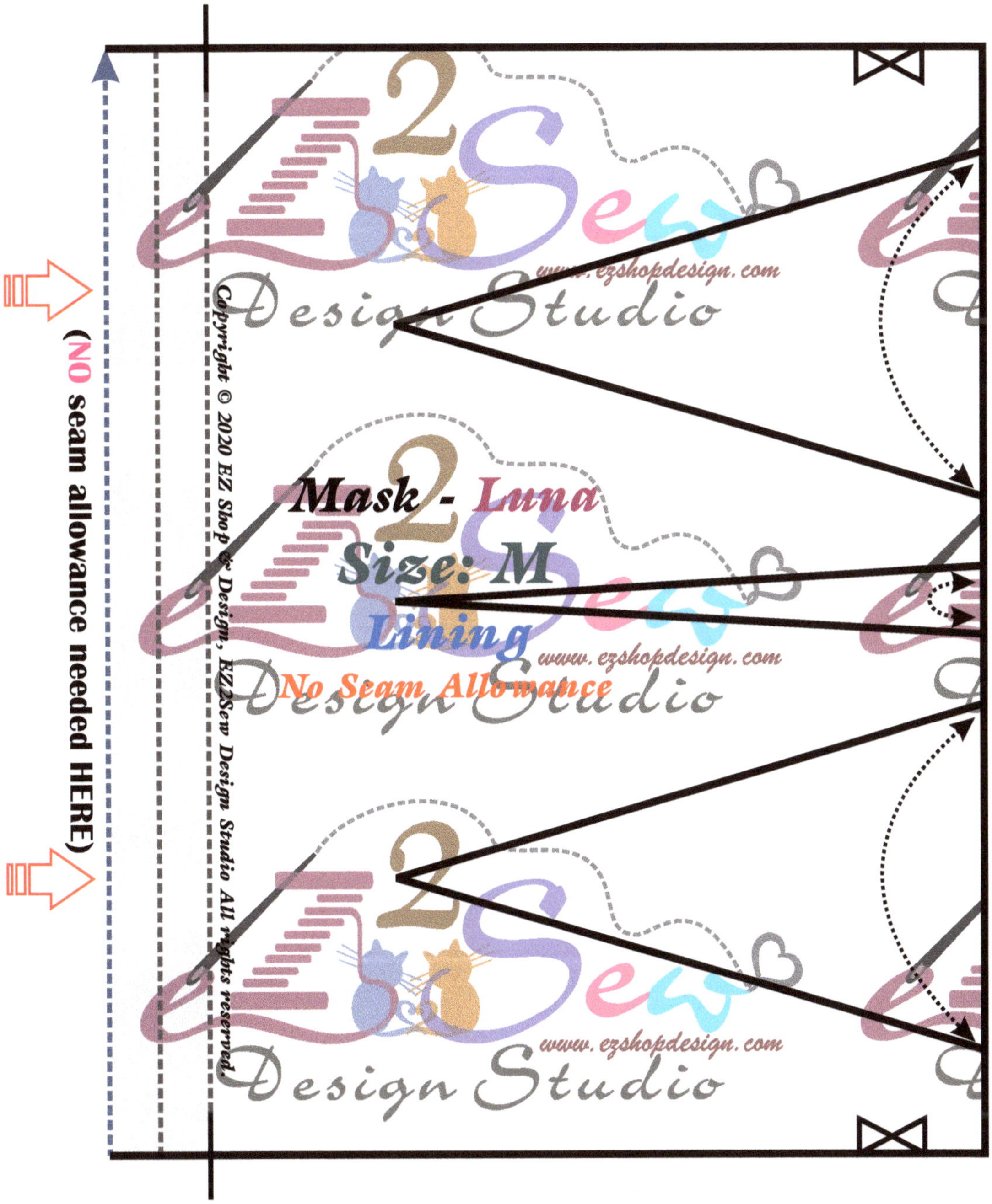

Mask - Luna
Size: M
Lining
No Seam Allowance

(NO seam allowance needed HERE)

92

PATTERN

Mask: Luna

Mask - Luna
Size: L
Main
No Seam Allowance

Copyright © 2020 EZ Shop & Hesi Jr, Ez2Sew Design Studio All rights reserved.

1"   3cm

93

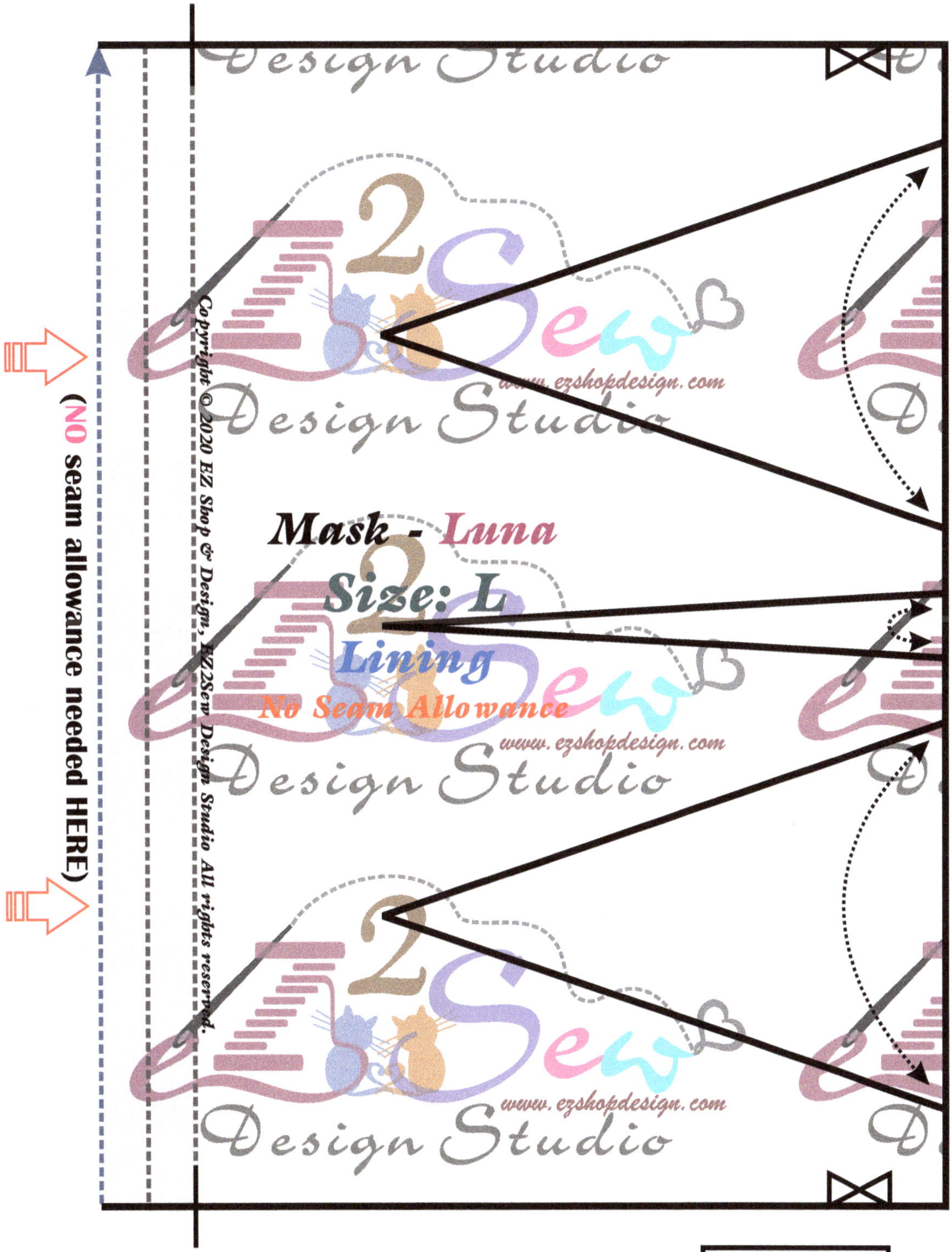

PATTERN

Mask: Luna

(**NO** seam allowance needed HERE)

Mask - Luna
Size: L
Lining
No Seam Allowance

1"   3cm

94

About the Author
Jacine Wang

She is a self-taught sewing creator and enjoys designing handbag patterns and sewing as well. While she is sewing, her two pretty kitties, Asti and Celine, are always on or under her sewing table, napping or playing, sometimes lying on the fabrics to get her attention while she works. They are her greatest influences and inspiration for her work. If she, who knew nothing about sewing, can sew, "sew" can you.

She has published two other books, "Sew Amazingly Cute" and "Sew Amazingly Elegant" recently. If you have any questions regarding these books, feel free to visit her web site www.jacinewang.com. She would love to hear from you and answer your questions.

Jacine lives in Plano, Texas with her husband, Charles; they have two kids, Christine and Johnathan and two cats, Asti and Celine.

"Sew Amazingly Cute"

"Sew Amazingly Elegant"

www.ingramcontent.com/pod-product-compliance
Lightning Source LLC
Chambersburg PA
CBHW042027100526
44587CB00029B/4323